Healthy Gluten-free Eating

Darina Allen   Rosemary Kearney

Healthy
Gluten-free
Eating

photography by Will Heap

Kyle Cathie Limited

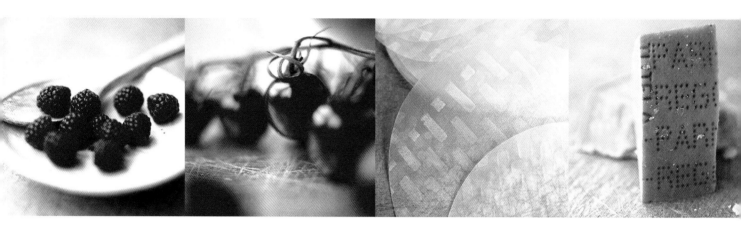

For Helen with love (Darina Allen)

For my mother Rosemary (1938–1980) who inspired me to cook. (Rosemary Kearney)

Acknowledgements

Darina, 14 books later, is still writing in longhand, despite annual New Year resolutions to learn to use the word processor, so a very special thank you to Truus Boelhouwer who meticulously typed the manuscript with endless patience and good humour.

Darina would also like to thank all the Ballymaloe Cookery School team for ongoing inspiration and support. And last but certainly not least, the indomitable Kyle Cathie for encouragement and friendship for many years.

Rosemary Kearney: Thanks to my family and friends for all their help and encouragement. A special thank you to my father Séamus, my husband Noel and my son Séamus for their love and support.

Thanks also to:
Annie Nichols, who cooked so deliciously and styled the food.
Will Heap for his gorgeous photos.
Ace editor Stephanie Horner.
Carl Hodson for his inspired design.
Muna Reyal for her sweet cajoling.

Coeliac disease is a chronic and permanent auto-immune disease caused by gluten intolerance. Gluten is a protein found in wheat, barley, oats and rye. When a person with coeliac disease eats gluten, even in minute quantities, it causes damage and inflammation to the gut, preventing normal digestion and absorption of food. When gluten is eliminated from the diet the gut returns to normal so the gluten free diet is the key to good health.

Latest estimates suggest that coeliac disease affects at least 1:100 people, yet fewer than 1:1000 are diagnosed. Diagnosis is quite simple, but many people are missed because they change their diet before the tests, so they end up with an inconclusive result. Because the diet is the treatment for coeliac disease, the markers used in diagnosis normalise once the diet is started, so you may end up with a false negative result. In other cases the symptoms are not identified because they vary from one person to another and can be anything from tiredness and anaemia to full-blown gut symptoms. Diagnosis involves a blood test that can be done by your local doctor followed by a gut biopsy that needs to be done by a gastroenterologist at the local hospital.

When you are first diagnosed with coeliac disease you may feel as though life will never be the same again. No more freshly baked bread or croissants. How about eating out or going to friends for a meal? What you need is a fresh approach to eating, focusing on the wealth of naturally gluten-free foods that are readily available. *Healthy Gluten-free Eating* is a personal account in which the authors use natural, organic ingredients in preference to processed or convenience versions. There is no doubt that coeliacs have to be aware of processed foods in terms of gluten status as when ingredients are added to products there is a possibility that a gluten-containing ingredient will also be added. However, we all use processed or convenience foods, from time to time, and there is nothing wrong with balancing the choices available – as long as they're gluten free!

As a charity, Coeliac UK provides information and advice to 60,000 members and anyone concerned they may have coeliac disease. We recommend that you should always consult with your doctor if you have any symptoms of coeliac disease. If you are diagnosed you need to obtain a referral to a dietitian for individualised advice.

Coeliac UK is a charity funded almost entirely by donations. We aim to improve the lives of individuals with coeliac disease and dermatitis herpetiformis by improving symptom awareness, diagnosis and management. We link with government agencies in order to raise awareness of the issues and we produce a range of resources, including *The Gluten-Free Food and Drink Directory* that lists over 11,000 foods. An interactive version is available at www.coeliacegg.co.uk. Other services include a thrice-yearly magazine, a diet helpline and over 90 support groups around the country.

To find out more about Coeliac UK, visit www.coeliac.co.uk
Coeliac UK
PO Box 220, High Wycombe, Bucks, HP11 2HY

Introduction to Coeliac Disease

Don't panic… that's the first and main thing if you have been recently diagnosed with coeliac disease.

People often think: What am I going to eat? No more bread, pasta, cakes, biscuits… the list seems endless. It doesn't have to be like this – take a step back and look at the wider picture. You have been diagnosed with a disease whereby you don't need to take tablets or receive injections because it is treatable – or rather controllable – by the food you eat. If anything, being diagnosed with coeliac disease can be a good thing for some people as it can make them realise how much processed food they may have been consuming! Therefore, it's time to get back to basics, using natural ingredients, and being responsible for the food we are eating in order to sustain healthy bodies.

Healthy eating for coeliacs need not mean tasteless, boring meals – no one has to compromise on flavour just because gluten has to be excluded from the diet and it need not lessen your pleasure in cooking and eating. Rather, see it as a fresh beginning – an opportunity to try new ingredients and a wide and more exciting range of recipes.

What exactly is coeliac disease?

Years ago, it was felt that coeliac disease was a childhood disease, one that you would grow out of. It is now known, however, that it is a permanent condition – one that you are born with (although it can strike at any age) and something that you do not 'grow out of' – and that it can affect people at any age. Chances are that if you have been diagnosed with coeliac disease, you will already know or have experienced at first hand either mild or chronic symptoms and undergone clinical tests to confirm the suspected gluten intolerance. However, if you are a not a coeliac and are about to embark upon cooking for a coeliac you may not realise the extent of this condition.

Coeliac disease is a genetic disease. It due to a permanent intolerance to gluten. Gluten is the name given to a number of different proteins (gliadin is the protein found in wheat, hordein is the protein in barley, secalin is the protein in rye and avenin is the protein in oats) which cause the immune reaction in coeliacs. It is gluten that gives bread its elasticity and cakes their spring. Unfortunately, even the tiniest amount of gluten can cause problems for coeliacs, despite the fact that individuals may not always be aware of the symptoms.

Coeliac disease is an autoimmune disease, resulting in gluten intolerance. The gluten damages an area in the small intestine, causing inflammation and subsequent malabsorption of food and nutrients. The only treatment required, though, to enable the intestine to return to normal and the painful effects of gluten intolerance to cease is to follow a completely gluten-free diet.

The link with diabetes

It is widely known that coeliac disease runs in families – there is an increased risk of one in ten where coeliac disease already exists. There is also an increased risk of other autoimmune diseases, which may occur alongside it, among them Type 1 diabetes. With this form of diabetes, the body is unable to regulate its blood sugar level due to an inability to produce the hormone insulin.

If someone has either coeliac disease or Type 1 diabetes, they are more likely to develop the other condition than people who don't have either. There is an increased risk of other autoimmune diseases associated with coeliac disease including hyperthyroidism. There is also a slightly higher risk of gut cancers and lymphomas in coeliac disease. However the biggest problem associated with coeliac disease is the reduced absorption of food, particularly nutrients such as iron and calcium, resulting in anaemia and osteoporosis respectively.

Symptoms of Coeliac Disease

Typical symptoms of coeliac disease

- Chronic tiredness
- Lethargy
- Headache
- Nausea
- Vomiting
- Bloating and cramps
- Diarrhoea
- Anaemia
- Mouth ulcers
- Thyroid problems
- Type 1 diabetes
- Osteopenia and osteoporosis
- Delayed or stunted growth in children / poor weight gain
- Weight loss
- Problems with fertility and pregnancy

The small intestine of the body is lined with millions of long, slender projections called villi, whose function among other things is to increase the surface area for absorption of food and nutrients – thereby enabling nutrients to be absorbed from the food we eat. Normally, these villi stand end-on-end, but in coeliac disease the body's immune response causes the villi in the small intestine to be flattened so that the surface area is greatly reduced. This results in malabsorption of nutrients and associated problems including anaemia and osteoporosis.

Tiredness as a result of malnutrition is very common in newly diagnosed coeliac disease, due to chronic poor iron absorption. There is also a problem with calcium absorption, resulting in osteoporosis. It is recommended that newly diagnosed coeliacs should have a bone density test to assess the degree of the problem and to treat as necessary.

Undiagnosed coeliac disease can result in infertility in both men and women and there is also an increased risk of miscarriage.

The symptoms of coeliac disease are variable and wide-ranging as people have differing sensitivities to gluten. As a result coeliac disease can be under-diagnosed or misdiagnosed for other illnesses such as irritable bowel syndrome.

Avoidance of gluten and any gluten-containing ingredients prevents damage to the lining of the small intestine and provides a complete treatment for the disease.

Diagnosis

Screening for coeliac disease is by means of a simple blood test to detect the presence of antibodies produced by coeliacs in response to gluten. It is then necessary to have a jejunal biopsy to examine the appearance of the lining or the villi of the small intestine under the microscope to check for damage.

No one who thinks that they may have the coeliac condition would be advised to start a gluten-free diet before being clinically diagnosed. If an individual embarks on a gluten-free diet before the condition is confirmed, their villi will show signs of repair and it will be difficult for the gastroenterologist to diagnose conclusively that coeliac disease may be the problem.

The final diagnosis of coeliac disease often brings about a sigh of relief. Many suffer for years before they find out why they felt so awful and are relieved to learn it was nothing more sinister. Now, they can do something about it.

Associated Conditions

Wheat intolerance versus gluten intolerance

Nowadays, a number of people consider that they are wheat intolerant. Allergy testing is widely available and many individuals may have been advised that they are wheat intolerant on the basis of a simple test that is performed without any medical supervision.

Food intolerance, and wheat intolerance in particular, is rare. If you suspect that you are wheat intolerant, you should be tested for coeliac disease before changing as wheat intolerance may mask the disease. It is more likely to affect young children and be a temporary problem. Symptoms may include skin problems including eczema. Simple food intolerance that is neither allergic nor coeliac disease may cause a variety of symptoms, including skin irritation, but does not affect the immune system.

Coeliac disease affects at least 1 per cent of the population and there is a clear diagnostic procedure which needs to be undertaken in the event of any symptoms being apparent.

The wheat-free diet is less restrictive than the gluten-free diet because a number of other grains can be ingested without ill effect, among them oats, rye and barley.

One word of warning here: not all food that is labelled as gluten-free is automatically safe for wheat-intolerant people. Commercially made gluten-free mixes, for instance, may contain a gluten-free wheat starch that is deemed to be safe for coeliacs, because the gluten has been removed, but, as the product is not wheat-free, it is still unsuitable for anyone with a wheat intolerance. Some people with coeliac disease are also not able to tolerate the special wheat-starch products. All the recipes in this collection use flours from pure gluten-free sources. They do not involve using commercial mixes which may contain this gluten-free wheat starch, and are therefore safe for coeliacs who follow the wheat-free and gluten-free diet.

The link between coeliac disease and lactose intolerance

There is a link between coeliac disease and lactose intolerance. When the gut is inflamed, as in newly diagnosed or untreated coeliac disease, there is a deficiency of the lactases (the enzymes that digest and absorb lactose – the sugar in milk). This is because the lactases are housed in the villi, which are flattened and reduced in coeliac disease.

Symptoms similar to coeliac disease may occur in associated lactose intolerance, including bloating, cramps and diarrhoea. To minimise these symptoms the individual must limit the amount of dairy products containing lactose he or she consumes. Most individuals can tolerate a small amount of milk in drinks and also cheese and yogurt to some extent. Many people find that once they have been following the gluten-free diet and the gut is less inflamed, they are able to tolerate milk products again. So, the lactose intolerance is generally a temporary problem.

With others, however, the lactose intolerance may be a permanent genetic problem and care must be taken that alternative foods containing a rich source of calcium are included in the diet. As with vegans, a registered dietitian should be consulted to assess your needs and give you specific advice.

The benefit of a coeliac diet for those who suffer from Dermatitis herpetiformis

Dermatitis herpetiformis (DH) is a condition in which a rash develops like little blisters on certain areas of the body, mainly on the knees, elbows and buttocks. This is also a result of a sensitivity to gluten and the digestive system may be affected too, giving rise to a form of coeliac disease.

DH is extremely itchy and therefore uncomfortable, and treatment is with the gluten-free diet.

Cereals and Grains that Contain Gluten

The following grains should be strictly avoided by coeliacs:

Wheat
Barley
Rye
Oats
Spelt

There is some uncertainty as to whether oats are suitable for coeliacs. Oats contain gluten, but oat gluten is from a different family of grains from barley and wheat. It is not clear whether pure oats cause damage to coeliacs, and some coeliacs may be able to tolerate a small quantity of oats, but the grain is still best avoided because it is very difficult to obtain oats that are totally free from contamination by wheat either in the field or in the milling process.

Spelt is a grain that is naturally low in gluten, but not gluten free, so it too should be avoided by coeliacs altogether.

You must remember 'wheat free' is NOT the same as 'gluten free'. I have seen bread that has been advertised as 'wheat free – suitable for coeliacs'. However, upon closer inspection, the main ingredient turned out to be rye flour. It is not rude to question exactly what the bread is made out of – and it is surely far better to take a few minutes to do this than to be buckled over in pain later that night, searching your brain trying to remember if you ate anything different – we have all been there, but we should try to avoid it!

Food labelling

In the past, poor labelling by food manufacturers often made it difficult for coeliacs to know if the product was safe for them to eat. The terms used can be confusing as they may not be obvious.

However, labelling is changing all the time and a new European Directive is making it obligatory for EU manufacturers to identify the presence of allergens like gluten in foods. By the end of 2005 it will be necessary for manufacturers to list all ingredients in foods and highlight the presence of 12 particular allergenic ingredients, including wheat and gluten.

In the meantime, some terms can be confusing because they may not be specific enough. They may not, for example, state which cereal is used in the manufacture. Indeed, the term 'starch' could mean starch made from wheat, barley or rye, in which case it should be avoided, but if it is made from potato, rice, tapioca or any other naturally gluten-free source, it is safe to eat. Unless you are sure of which starch is used, it is best to avoid it.

Ready meals, tinned, packaged and processed foods may contain flour as a processing, binding or thickening agent, as might gravies, sauces and batter.

There are many other instances where there may be gluten present.

Some home bakeries provide gluten-free bread that they have made on their premises, but unless it has been made in a completely separate environment, contamination is a high risk.

Terms used by manufacturers that indicate the presence of gluten

- Barley starch
- Binder
- Bran
- Bulgur, cracked wheat
- Cereal
- Cereal protein
- Couscous
- Durum wheat
- Fillers
- Flour
- Kamut
- Malt
- Malted barley
- Oat bran
- Oat germ
- Oatmeal
- Pearl barley
- Porridge oats
- Rolled oats
- Rusk
- Rye starch
- Semolina
- Thickener
- Triticale (a mixture of wheat and rye)
- Vegetable gum
- Vegetable starch
- Wheat bran
- Wheat germ
- Wheat meal
- Wheat rusk
- Wheat starch

Butchers who provide products such as gluten-free sausages must also be aware of how important it is that these are made without cross-contamination as sausages normally contain a cereal binder or filler. Likewise, you need to wary of any product made using ready-made spices mixes or flavourings as these may well contain a percentage of flour.

Coeliac UK and The Coeliac Society of Ireland produce a list of gluten-free food, so be guided by their recommended products (see pages 15 and 30). Many coeliac societies in other countries also publish such a directory.

Simple precautions to adopt at home

There are a few things to get in the habit of doing in your own kitchen. Store gluten-free flours, for example, well separate from regular flour – in separate tins to avoid any risk of contamination. Similarly, don't put your gluten-free biscuits in the same tin with regular biscuits – you could be easily eating crumbs that contain gluten.

You should set up a separate toaster, bread board and butter or spread dish in order to ensure you minimise the risk of contamination from regular breadcrumbs. Make sure you use separate cutlery and utensils for butter, jams and spreads for the same reason. And don't forget to wash your hands and nails thoroughly and to change your apron if you have been cooking with regular flour before you begin to cook food for a coeliac.

The following foods and drinks may include gluten without you realising it

- Baking powder
- Communion wafers
- 'Corn tortillas' may also contain regular flour
- Frozen chips – flour may be present to keep them white
- Stock cubes / powder
- Vegetable soup may contain pearl barley
- White pepper may be 'bulked' with flour
- Inferior brands of ground almonds may contain breadcrumbs
- Seasoning mixes
- Mustard powder
- Packet suet may have flour in it to stop it sticking together
- Packets of ready-grated cheese may contain flour
- Cheese spreads
- Commercial salad dressings and mayonnaise
- Soy sauce (there are gluten-free brands available, e.g. Japanese tamari)
- Dry-roasted nuts
- Pretzels
- Bombay mix
- Scotch eggs
- Food that has been deep–fried with other gluten-containing food, e.g. battered fish and chips

- Processed meats, e.g. ham, may be injected with a cereal 'filler' to increase their protein content or thinly sliced meats may also have 'fillers'
- Flavoured crisps
- Some fizzy drinks (alcoholic or non-alcoholic) may contain barley flour to give a cloudy appearance. Always check the source
- Coffee from vending machines
- Malted milk drinks
- Barley water or flavoured barley water
- Beer, lager, stout and ale are all made from grain
- Some tablets contain flour as a binder or filler
- Children's 'pick & mix' sweets may be coated in flour to stop them from sticking together
- Brightly coloured modelling dough used by children is not a food, but strangely enough it can sometimes get into their little mouths and you should be aware that it is made from wheat flour
- Check all brands and processed foods as they may contain added ingredients that are not gluten-free

Much of this hidden gluten is contained in processed foods – which is another good reason for coeliacs and non-coeliacs alike to cook with fresh, natural ingredients.

The Gluten-free Food List

It is crucial that coeliacs, especially those newly diagnosed, are familiar with the foods that they can eat. Many coeliac societies produce a directory of approved products. Coeliac UK and The Coeliac Society of Ireland produce *The Food and Drink Directory* as a guide to gluten-free food and drink. They list branded and own-label gluten-free products by manufacturers who have confirmed that these products meet the current standard for gluten free, as set by the international body, Codex Alimentarius. As products and recipes change throughout the year, it is imperative that you keep your Directory updated on a monthly basis. You should also be sure to refer to your local Registered Dietitian and health-care team for specific guidance on your gluten-free diet and your individual tolerance of Codex wheat starch, malt extract and oats.

The importance of sticking to a gluten-free diet

Once gluten has been removed from the diet, the symptoms should subside within days, but the small intestine may take six months to two years to heal. As people have differing sensitivities to gluten, one person may break their diet and feel fine whereas another may eat gluten and have a very rapid and painful response. If anything, this should put you off breaking your diet and you will tend to be very strict with yourself thereafter. The problem with breaking your diet and not feeling the ill-effects is that you are nevertheless doing continual damage to your small intestine. Therefore, in order to keep the symptoms under control and to prevent any further complications, it is vital that all gluten – even the tiniest proportion – is permanently removed from the diet. If you stick to a strict gluten-free diet, you should absorb nutrients, but if you become complacent and break the diet, the villi will remain damaged and as a result you may not absorb all the nutrients you need from your food to be healthy. In short, the small intestine will not heal to its full potential unless gluten is permanently removed from the diet.

Remember, though: you are never cured from coeliac disease even if the symptoms disappear, but it is something you can learn to manage.

Coeliacs and alcohol

Beers, lagers, stouts and real ales must definitely be avoided, but wine, champagne, port, sherry, liqueurs, spirits, including whisky and malt whisky, and cider – are all gluten-free.

Foods that are gluten-free

- All fresh meat and fish
- All fresh fruit and vegetables
- Fresh herbs and plain/individual spices
- Corn and cornmeal (maize/sweetcorn)
- Dried peas, lentils, pulses and beans
- Rice and wild rice
- Rice bran
- Rice noodles
- Plain nuts and seeds
- Eggs
- Dairy products – milk, cream, natural yogurt, cheese
- Soya and tofu
- Sugar
- Honey
- Golden syrup
- Maple syrup
- Treacle
- Jams and marmalade
- Pure oils and fats
- Vinegars
- Tomato purée
- Vanilla essence and extract
- Fresh and dried yeast

Gluten-free Alternatives

Naturally gluten-free cereals and grains

Rest assured there is a wide range of naturally gluten-free cereals available. Truth be told they are not as easily worked with as regular flour, but I have familiarised myself with them – resulting in recipes that I hope you will find enjoyable. The following cereals and flours are naturally 'gluten-free':

- Rice flour
- Tapioca flour/cassava flour
- Potato flour
- Cornflour
- Ground cornmeal (polenta)
- Soya flour
- Gram flour/chickpea flour
- Chestnut flour
- Buckwheat flour
- Lotus root flour
- Carob flour
- Millet flour
- Quinoa flour
- Sorghum
- Arrowroot
- Linseed
- Sago
- Teff

You still need to exercise great care when purchasing these flours. Ensure you are buying good-quality brands, which have meticulous policies regarding cross contamination (see the suppliers list on page 157 and check your Directory). Some flours may be gluten-free but may be milled in a factory that mills gluten-containing flours. There is always a risk of cross contamination if you are unsure of your source of flour!

There is no reason why coeliacs should feel they are missing out on certain foods. The aim of this book is to enable you to cook recipes that you may have seen on menus and longed to try or, if you were diagnosed later in life, used to enjoy. The recipes are formulated using natural sources of gluten-free flours. There are many commercial gluten-free mixes available if you cannot find these gluten-free flours. However, not all brands give the same result and it is difficult to write recipes that are standard for all gluten-free flour mixes.

The range of foods available is certainly expanding, together with increasing awareness among the general public and within the food industry. The dried gluten-free pasta available, including corn pasta and rice pasta, is wonderful and there are several organic brands that are worth trying.

Don't forget about rice noodles – they are practically an instant food and by using them you can have a meal ready in a matter of minutes. Rice paper wrappers (see photograph) are great for 'wraps' in place of flour tortillas. And instead of a wheat-based soy sauce, look out for Japanese tamari soy sauce, which is made from soya beans and rice rather than wheat flour (but always check the brand in your Directory – see page 15).

Poppadums are gluten-free and are great with gluten-free Indian meals, but it would be advisable to check the ingredients list just in case, for example, a spice mix has been added to them. Also ensure they are cooked in a wok or deep-fat fryer that hasn't been contaminated with gluten from other flours.

I find it useful to bake a loaf of gluten-free white soda bread especially to make into breadcrumbs. I then freeze batches of crumbs in small quantities so that I have them ready to use at my convenience. They are so useful for stuffings, fishcakes, coated chicken fillets… in fact anything that calls for breadcrumbs can be made gluten-free. Of course, you can use any of the plain breads, but I find the white soda bread is quickest and most convenient.

Xanthan gum

A relatively new product that I have found indispensable for baking is xanthan gum. Naturally gluten-free flours are less elastic in texture. Adding a small amount of xanthan gum will, to some extent, replace these elastic qualities. The gum is an invaluable aid for gluten-free cooking and should be on every coeliac's shopping list!

Xanthan gum is now available in the special dietary section of some of the major supermarket retailers. Health food stores that stock a comprehensive range of good-quality gluten-free products should also supply it. Failing that, you can order it directly from the manufacturer, found under the list of suppliers at the end of this book.

A Balanced Diet

A healthy, wholesome diet for everyone, coeliacs and non-coeliacs alike, is of utmost importance. The coeliac diet can, and has the potential to be, one of the healthiest diets around because of the increased emphasis placed upon eating fresh, natural and unadulterated food. Consumers generally are made more aware of what actually goes into processed food by constantly reading the food labels. Everyone is waking up to the fact that there are preservatives and additives in many foods that we could all do without. Convenience foods also tend to have high fat, salt and sugar levels, so we should try to avoid them as well. Top-quality, naturally produced food free from pesticides and additives is what we should all strive to consume. Better still, buy organic, locally produced food if at all possible. Find out as much as you can about the provenance of the food and where and how it was produced.

As with any other sensible diet you need to maintain a balance between the proportions of protein, fibre, fats and carbohydrate. Everything in moderation is the key, and by using the freshest and best ingredients available, along with adopting good cooking practices, we coeliacs can ensure we are getting adequate vitamins and minerals.

As nutritional deficiencies are symptomatic of undiagnosed coeliac disease, your local medical team may encourage you to take a supplement – it is therefore essential to get advice from properly qualified medical personnel, as everybody has different requirements. This is particularly the case when assessing the need for iron or calcium supplements.

Fruit and vegetables

We should aim to eat at least five portions of fruit and vegetables a day as they are important sources of essential vitamins and minerals as well as fibre. Aim to eat about 400g (14oz) a day. A portion (80g/3oz) can consist of:

- one banana, apple or orange
- a large slice of a large fruit, such as melon or pineapple
- two small fruits such as kiwis, plums, clementines or satsumas, or a small bunch of grapes
- two tablespoons of vegetables (whether raw, cooked, frozen or tinned), but potatoes should not be included as they are starchy carbohydrates
- one small glass of fresh fruit juice
- ½–1 tablespoon of dried fruit
- 2–3 tablespoons of fresh or tinned fruit salad
- 1 dessert bowl of salad

Try to eat a variety of fruit and vegetables. Leafy vegetables are a good source of iron and folate, both of which are important in preventing anaemia. Fruit and vegetables also contain magnesium and phosphorus, essential for bone health, as well as antioxidants such as vitamins C and E, which will help to protect against heart disease and cancer.

Fibre

It is widely recognised that a diet high in fibre is vital for healthy gut function. Many people obtain their fibre from eating wholegrain bread and cereals. However, for coeliacs this can be a difficulty, as a number of cereals which are a good source of fibre must be eliminated from the gluten-free diet. Coeliacs therefore need to ensure that they are obtaining their fibre requirement from other rich sources, such as rice bran, brown rice and legumes (beans, peas and pulses) as well as fresh fruit and vegetables. Dried fruits, nuts and seeds can also make valuable contributions to a healthy diet.

The question of fat

Not all fat is bad – not only does it add flavour to the food we eat, but it also provides us with the fat-soluble vitamins A, D, E and K. A little fat in moderation is perfectly acceptable in a healthy diet, but we need to know which fats are better than others.

Olive and rapeseed oil are rich in monounsaturates and should therefore be used in preference over other oils for both cooking and in dressings.

Everyone should choose poly-unsaturated and monounsaturated fats in favour of saturated fats and trans fats. Found chiefly in animal and dairy products, saturated fats have a major influence on cholesterol levels in the blood. Trans fats are mainly products of a process called hydrogenation, which is used to make unsaturated fats firm and spreadable. They are found in spreads and bakery products and can also raise cholesterol. Look for products that are labelled as free from trans fats.

Omega-3 and omega-6 fats are derived from the essential fatty acids. Linoleic and alpha-linolenic acid are two types of fatty acid found in polyunsaturated fats and are essential for good health and especially to help protect against heart disease. Good sources of omega-3 fats include oily fish, such as halibut and mackerel, rapeseed oil, olive oil, soya beans and green leafy vegetables, all of which are suitable for coeliacs.

Butter and lard both contain saturated fats. If you want to limit your consumption of these, you can cut down by spreading a thinner layer of butter on your bread or dipping it in olive oil, or switch to using olive or groundnut oil in cooking or frying instead.

Protein and carbohydrate

Good rich sources of protein are vital for the maintenance, growth and repair of the body. Wonderful sources of protein are pulses, e.g. lentils, chickpeas; animal sources, e.g. meat, dairy products; and nuts – and all of them are gluten free. There are numerous recipes in this book which will supply you with rich sources of protein at every meal, so why not start your day on the right footing with a bowl of gluten-free muesli topped with plenty of cashew nuts and hazelnuts and low-fat milk or organic natural yogurt?

The gluten-free diet tends to be higher in protein than a normal diet because of the number of cereals that are restricted and it is therefore important for the gluten-free diet to include gluten-free carbohydrates as the main energy sources – fruit, brown rice, buckwheat and millet, pulses and maize as well as gluten-free pasta and cereals.

Carbohydrates are made up of sugars and starches. It is important to include more high-fibre starchy foods and base meals around foods such as gluten-free pasta, gluten-free bread, potatoes, rice and polenta. Cut down on sweets and sugary foods if you are trying to lose weight or worried about dental health.

Cooking for a Coeliac

Don't be filled with dread at the thought of cooking for a coeliac – the recipes in this book are no more challenging than cooking normally. The reality is that there really is no need to cook two different dishes if you are catering for a coeliac family member or guest because gluten-free meals can be just as delicious, particuarly when meals are made from naturally gluten-free foods.

True, some planning is required as you may not be able to get all the special flours in your local supermarket, but you will be surprised at how little extra effort you need. A tasty piece of pan-fried fish tossed in rice flour, or a curry with gluten-free naan bread will be appreciated. (Remember to avoid contamination while cooking. For example, if you are making gluten-free pastry, use a gluten-free flour to roll out the dough and keep all cooking utensils and cutlery away from gluten sources (see page 13.)

Speak to your guest in advance, clarifying what they cannot eat. It can be very embarrassing for both the host and guest if there is nothing suitable on the menu, but when at the dinner table don't make an issue of your guest being different. This will ensure that you all have a relaxing evening – remember that entertaining should be enjoyable.

One good tip – if you have been invited to a party and are unsure what food will be available, eat beforehand, and if there are nibbles you can eat it will be a bonus. If there is nothing suitable, at least you won't be ravenous by the time you get home.

Feeding the Family

Babies

It is recommended that gluten should not be introduced into the weaning process of any baby until the baby is six months old. This minimises the risk of intolerance. Breast feeding is always recommended, if possible. Puréed vegetables, baby rice and fruit purées are great first foods. After six months you can introduce gluten, but if there is a history of coeliac disease, be extra vigilant for the baby showing any signs of the associated symptoms. If you have any concerns, consult your doctor as soon as possible.

Children

It is essential that you consult your local medical team regularly for specific advice on diet during childhood to ensure that dietary requirements for growth and development are met.

It can be difficult for coeliac children to understand that there are just some foods that they cannot have, no matter how much they may want them. However, in these instances it really is a case of having to be cruel to be kind; giving in and letting them eat, for instance, a regular biscuit is not doing them any favours. Whether or not your child shows any symptoms of being ill as a result of eating that one biscuit is not the point – the child's small intestine is being damaged and this can in turn lead to more serious long-term problems.

Carefully explain and educate your child about the importance of eating only certain types of food and checking if they are unsure. Family members and close friends should also have the condition explained to them so that they do not unconsciously give your child gluten-containing treats.

Your child's school and youth groups should be informed of your child's condition. Certain schools may provide a gluten-free meal, but if not, a tasty packed lunch will keep them satisfied. Years ago, gluten-free bread was available in tins and my friends (and myself for that matter) found it very hard to understand why my sandwiches were round!

It is very important at this early age that your child is not made to feel different or left out of things just because they can't eat certain foods. Don't make a fuss that a child cannot eat certain foods. This will only make feel them embarrassed in front of their peers. The child must be made aware of how important it is that they do not sneak any of the forbidden foods, such as certain sweets or biscuits, when no one is looking. I was no angel when I was a child and had a weakness for chocolate-coated biscuit fingers. I was caught on more than one occasion trying to cram as many biscuit fingers into my mouth as possible before my parents could pounce out of their seats faster than a sprinter to force them out of my mouth!

That is not to say that coeliac children cannot have treats: there are plenty of options available. Birthday parties are a huge event in a child's life – when they are invited to a friend's party, contact the family in advance and maybe drop round a special food goody-bag so that your child does not feel left out when all the other friends are filling their faces with birthday cake. If you are holding the birthday party, why not have everything on the menu suitable for coeliacs – then no one need know the difference and your child is free to eat what they like without having to check with you on the big day.

Pregnancy

This topic is fresh in my mind as my three-month-old son gurgles on my knee! Again, you should refer to your local health-care team for specific advice on diet and health. It is recommended that all pregnant women take folic acid supplements before and during pregnancy. This is of extreme importance for coeliac mums-to-be, as they are more susceptible to folic acid deficiency. Always consult your doctor before taking extra supplements, though, to ensure you do not take more than is recommended – too high levels may be endangering you and your baby.

During pregnancy, women are more aware of the extra nutritional demands on their bodies. It is of particular importance in coeliac disease to eat a well-balanced, healthy diet. Morning sickness can make you feel as if you've been indulging in piles of gluten-containing foods, but don't ever be tempted to eat regular biscuits or cakes to satisfy those cravings!

Vegetarians and vegans

As a coeliac diet is already severely restrictive, vegetarian coeliacs need to take extra care to avoid increasing the risk of nutritional deficiencies and you should always refer to your local health-care team for specific guidance. Since milk and milk products are the prime source of calcium in the diet, veganism, where all animal products are cut out, can severely restrict calcium intake when requirements are high. But with careful planning it is possible to eat a healthy, balanced vegetarian/vegan coeliac diet.

Anaemia is common in coeliac disease, so sources of iron including pulses, eggs, fortified gluten-free breads and dark greens are essential. There may be increased requirements for vitamins B12 and folic acid, also associated with anaemia. Fermented soya products, seaweeds, and algae such as spirulina, may contain significant B12. Many vegan foods are supplemented with B12 but may not be gluten free. Liver, yeast extract, vegetables and fortified cereal products are good sources of folic acid.

Alternative sources of protein are soya foods including tofu, tempeh and textured vegetable protein. There are also various soya dairy alternatives. Tofu is a source of calcium. Silken tofu is soft and creamy and can be used in dips and sauces, while firm tofu can be marinated. Quorn is another good source of protein and iron that is used in vegetarian diets. Gluten-free cereals also provide B-vitamins, protein and carbohydrates.

Eating Out

Years ago, very few people had heard about coeliac disease. This lack of awareness made it difficult for coeliacs to feel comfortable about eating in restaurants. However, times have changed and nowadays people within the food industry and the food service sector are more aware about coeliac disease. Many chefs and restaurants are only too willing to cater for coeliacs and offer them gluten-free alternative options.

There are a few basic guidelines if you are eating out that will make life easier and more enjoyable for yourself.

First, it is advisable to ring the restaurant in advance and if possible try to speak to the chef. Good restaurants that make all their meals from fresh ingredients on the premises will be able to tell you exactly what is in each dish. Other restaurants, however, may use ready-made sauces or powdered potatoes, for example. It is essential that they check with the manufacturer before confirming what is suitable for coeliacs.

The chef must be made aware of the severity of the problem and that it is not just a 'fad' diet! Don't hesitate to question what is in everything. The smallest amount of regular flour can be enough to cause problems for the coeliac.

If enough coeliacs put pressure on restaurants to provide gluten-free meals, more and more chefs will become aware of the condition and that can only be a good thing. Training must be given in catering establishments to teach up-and-coming chefs about the condition. Staff should not try to guess the content of dishes or give false assurances – ask them to check with the chef.

The coeliac customer must continually stress the importance of having no gluten in the food they are eating. For example, if you are ordering pan-fried fish, make sure it is not tossed in regular flour before it is cooked, and that there is no risk of cross contamination from the utensils being used for gluten-containing flours.

Other items on the menu can usually be adapted to suit coeliacs. A lot of soups are potato-based and are therefore naturally gluten-free. Check that the soup is not thickened with flour. Some dishes can usually be adapted, such as a Caesar salad (check that the dressing is gluten free) without the croûtons. If you are having a pasta dish and you are sure the sauce is 'safe' to eat, give the kitchen gluten-free pasta or rice noodles in advance. Don't forget to stress that your pasta needs to be cooked in fresh water and not in the water which was used to cook the regular pasta!

Provided you say so in advance, it is normally acceptable to bring your own gluten-free bread to a restaurant, but remember to let the manager know, so that there are no embarrassing confrontations when you take your parcel out of your bag.

Some very good restaurants have realised there is now a market for 'coeliac-friendly' meals and stress this on their menus. Some even go as far as providing gluten-free bread – these little extras are what I always remember about a restaurant and such restaurants always warrant a second visit!

On the dessert menu, there will be many options that will obviously contain gluten, such as pastries, but don't always take it for granted that other choices, ice creams or meringues, for instance, are automatically the safe option. Check once again that they are gluten-free. The chances are that if the ice cream has been bought in, it may contain flour, and those tempting-looking meringues may never have started off life as an egg white but instead have come out of a packet!

If you have a good local restaurant it may be worth building up a relationship with your chef – in a purely culinary sense! Eating out should be a pleasurable experience and you should not spend the night fretting about whether the food you are about to eat is suitable. If in doubt, leave it out – chances are that as you are the coeliac, you may be better informed about what you can and cannot eat than the chef, no matter how good his or her intentions are.

If you are buying meals or ingredients from food counters or delis, make sure that the serving staff do not cross contaminate your food by handling gluten-containing sources with their hands or tongs first.

Finally, when you're holidaying abroad, it is a good idea to see whether you can get someone to write a note in their native language, explaining the condition and the seriousness of it.

Fast-food outlets

Generally burgers, sausages and other prepared meats are not allowed. Question the chips, too. Frozen chips may be coated in flour, but if they have been prepared on the premises, there is a good chance they will be suitable. However, you must be 100 per cent sure that they are cooked in fresh oil which has not been used for cooking fried fish or French-fried onions. Even if they are not cooking with the chips and the oil has been subsequently filtered, there is still a high risk of gluten residues in the oil.

Italian restaurants

Once you have established what is gluten free, you can enjoy gorgeous creamy risottos with courgette flowers or porcini mushrooms and polenta with deliciously fresh toppings or oozing with Parmesan and Gorgonzola. I have enjoyed cold set polenta as an alternative to crusty breads for dipping into fruity olive oils. Don't forget the gorgeous array of salads that are suitable, such as tomato, mozzarella and fresh basil, which are normally dressed with an olive oil-based dressing, but beware of creamier dressing and remember, no croûtons. And there are plenty of vegetable main course options.

Indian restaurants

Believe it or not, there are suitable choices if you eat in an authentic Indian restaurant, where all the dishes are made from fresh, basic ingredients. If not, the dishes may be prepared from ready-made sauces, and the chef may not know if they contain flour. Also, if the chef uses fresh whole spices, he or she can be sure that the spices have not been adulterated and bulked with flour that may not be listed in the ingredients.

Many dishes in such good restaurants will thus be suitable, using natural yogurt in tandoori-style cooking or ground almonds to thicken kormas.

Plain boiled rice and pullao-type dishes are often a good bet, as are plain poppadoms – check the oil has not been used for deep frying gluten-containing food, or ask for yours to be grilled instead. Many of the meat and vegetarian curries will be acceptable, but always check as there may be a little flour added without you realising it.

Pakoras and onion bajis are usually made with chickpea (gram) flour, which is fine, but always double-check if they are suitable. There may be a tablespoon of regular flour added – enough to cause problems for the coeliac. Many of the dishes made from pulses such as dhals will be suitable for coeliacs and they are also wonderfully nutritious.

Forget about many of the Indian breads, such as poori, chapati and paratha. These are definitely off limits, as are samosas. However, you will find a recipe for gluten-free naan bread in this book and you could always eat this with your curries. Please remember to check if this is okay with the restaurateur beforehand – you don't want any embarrassing confrontations in the restaurant!

Chinese/Thai restaurants

The problem with eating in a Chinese or Thai restaurant is knowing which dishes contain soy sauce. Japanese tamari soy sauce, made from soya beans, is available on the market and is suitable for coeliacs, but most chefs will automatically use a wheat-based soy sauce. Alarm bells should ring in your ears! You may think that a little splosh here and there won't do you any harm, but there will be sufficient present to cause some degree of inflammation to the villi in the small intestine.

As with any restaurant, it's a question of trust. If you have a very understanding chef who is aware of the seriousness of giving a coeliac any gluten, he or she may well facilitate matters for you and use the gluten-free Japanese tamari soy sauce. Alternatively, if you can't be sure, you could always just ask that soy sauce is left out of your meal completely. Ask if you can bring your own gluten-free brand to flavour your food.

Look into the selection of rice dishes or go for rice noodles which are absolutely fine for coeliacs. Rice-wrapper spring rolls are a tasty alternative, instead of the more traditional spring rolls. Some dishes will be cooked with coconut milk, which is another option for coeliacs, or you could go for steamed fish or vegetables with ginger.

Prawn crackers are usually okay for coeliacs, but again you must be quite sure they are cooked in oil free from gluten residues.

Shopping for Gluten-free Food

There's no getting away from it: shopping for coeliacs does take a little bit of extra time. Buying fresh ingredients such as fruit and vegetables is not an issue, because you know these are suitable. However, you have to take a little more care over processed foods.

Ready-made sauces and other convenience foods may contain only a small proportion of flour (see the lists on pages 12 and 13); nonetheless it is there and as a result should be avoided at all costs – no matter how tempting it may seem! This is where your *Food and Drink Directory* comes into its own (see page 15) – use it to check that brands really are gluten free. It will give you a comprehensive guide to what is 'safe' to eat, but don't forget to get it regularly updated, at least on a monthly basis. The new EU Directive on food labelling (see page 12) will also make choosing food much easier and safer.

It's worth repeating that 'wheat free' and 'gluten free' are not interchangeable terms, so don't ever rely on this method of labelling.

Finding reliable sources of gluten-free ingredients

In the UK, between 2000 and 2002, the gluten-free market increased by about 400 per cent. Specialist gluten-free manufacturers now produce good ranges of ready-made sauces and meals. Many of the larger supermarkets now have specialist dietary sections which offer, among other items, gluten-free flour mixes and ready-made bread, cakes and biscuits. Some of the flours specified in this book may be found in these specialist sections, but others may not. Because there may not be sufficient demand for a specialist type of flour, a store may not stock it but it is up to us, as consumers, to request it time and time again so that the management may realise there is a market. If it turns out to be tricky to source gluten-free flours, good health-food stores, if they do not already stock all the types, should be able to order them for you without difficulty (see also the list of suppliers at the end of the book).

On that note, if your health-food store operates a serve-yourself policy, whereby you put the quantity of flour you want into a bag and it is then weighed, you must be absolutely certain that the scoop used for the gluten-free flours is not also used in the regular flours. Do stay alert to the dangers of cross contamination.

If you live close to an Asian foodstore or supermarket, you may find that they sell some of the flours, often in larger quantities. As always, you need to be sure that they come from 'pure' sources and are not contaminated with other flours.

Alternatively, several companies provide a mail-order service, or the gluten-free flours can now be purchased on-line via the Internet. (See the suppliers listed at the back of this book.)

In the UK, coeliacs can also obtain bread and flour mixes on prescription and other countries have their own arrangements for coeliacs.

Gluten-free snacks when you're on the move

If you're planning an extended shopping trip, it is always a good idea to take a gluten-free snack with you in case you decide to break for a cup of coffee, as is often the case when I shop with my sister. Not all cafés will have gluten-free goodies, so just mention why you've brought your own, otherwise they may not look kindly upon you eating food that was not purchased in their establishment. The other option, of course, in which you may think you are being very discreet, is to hide your gluten-free treat behind your napkin and try to eat it like this… blindingly obvious to everyone in the café but yourself!

Always take a supply of snacks and drinks (and avoid those from vending machines) if you are travelling for long periods – especially when you don't know what eating facilities will be available at airports, railway stations and so on. Although food choices are improving, you may still find that the only suitable food is a piece of fruit.

In response to many requests over a number of years, we put on the first course for coeliacs at the Ballymaloe Cookery School in the year 2000.

Our courses are invariably greeted with a positive and enthusiastic response from the participants, but on this occasion there was an extra element which really touched me – a deep gratitude. The students who participated in the course were thrilled to eat such delicious food, since many looked upon their diagnosis as a 'life sentence' of dull and unappetising meals, and were truly convinced that they would never be able to taste really yummy food ever again.

Instead Rosemary made them realise that this was an opportunity to embark on an altogether healthier wholefood diet, which certainly does not mean less flavour; rather, it offers a chance to broaden culinary horizons and discover new and tasty ingredients.

Rosemary adores cooking and it shows. She has spent long hours in her kitchen testing recipes to share with her fellow coeliacs. One in one hundred of the population is a coeliac and the numbers are increasing at an alarming rate, mainly as a result of increasing recognition. Catering for coeliacs is a considerable and growing market which chefs and restaurants too rarely consider when they are planning their menus. If only they knew how grateful coeliac diners are when they respond to their needs! The word spreads quickly and those that do respond will soon be inundated with eager excited coeliacs.

Where to begin…? You will need to stock up your store cupboard with coeliac products and become familiar with their use, so you can whip up some yummy meals in minutes. We have put together a list of products to keep in stock. However, in a household where just one person is coeliac, remember, if it's practical, to reserve a cupboard for their use alone.

Storecupboard ingredients

- Rice flour, tapioca flour, potato flour, cornflour, cornmeal, soya flour, gram flour, buckwheat flour
- Xanthan gum
- Bicarbonate of soda, gluten-free baking powder, cream of tartar
- Milk powder
- Lecithin (this comes from soya beans and is available from chemists or health food shops. It is rich in phosphatidyl choline, an important nutrient in the control of dietary fat which helps the body to convert fats into energy rather than storing them as body fat. Check that it is GM-free.)
- Dried active yeast
- Nuts, including ground almonds, pine nuts
- Millet flakes
- Rice bran, rice flakes
- Dried fruit
- Pure vanilla extract
- Rice
- Rice paper wrappers
- Rice noodles – fine, flat
- Gluten-free pasta – penne, lasagne, macaroni
- Dried pulses – beans/lentils, e.g. haricot beans/chickpeas
- Gluten-free icing sugar
- Best-quality dark chocolate – minimum 70 per cent cocoa solids
- Oils and vinegars, including sesame oil
- Dijon mustard
- Whole spices including black peppercorns/white peppercorns (ensure that you use pure white pepper or check your *Food and Drink Directory* as some brands are bulked with flour)
- Gluten-free Japanese tamari soy sauce
- Nam pla (fish sauce)
- Gluten-free poppadoms

And one final thing. A nutritional analysis is given at the end of each recipe, so if you are at all concerned about weight loss or health issues, please choose appropriately. For example, we think that it would be wrong to try to cut out all animal fat. The marbling of fat in beef, for instance, is necessary for us to enjoy meat which is succulent and tasty, while a nice layer of fat around pork is essential for sweet, juicy bacon. However, if you are concerned about fat, choose leaner cuts.

Perception is everything, and unfortunately few people expect coeliac food to be as good as regular food. Rosemary has proved that the opposite is true – and all these recipes can be enjoyed by all the family and friends. Some are suitable for quick and simple meals, others perfect for casual entertaining and even more sophisticated parties. All are delicious!

1

Breakfasts and Brunches

Granola

Homemade crunchy granola tastes delicious with ice-cold creamy milk and sliced banana and is a great way to provide you with all the energy you need to start the day off productively. **Serves 10**

175g (6oz) honey
125ml (4fl oz) sunflower oil
425g (15oz) rice flakes
110g (4oz) roasted buckwheat
110g (4oz) hazelnuts, split and roasted
75g (3oz) seedless raisins

40g (1½oz) rice bran
40g (1½oz) millet flakes
25g (1oz) ready-to-eat dried apricots or dates, chopped

To serve
Sliced banana

Preheat the oven to 180°C/350°F/gas mark 4.

Mix the honey and oil together in a saucepan. Heat just enough to melt the honey. Mix well into the rice flakes. Spread thinly on a baking sheet and bake in the oven for 20–30 minutes, turning frequently and making sure the edges do not burn. The mixture should be golden and toasted, and not roasted!

Cool and mix in the buckwheat, hazelnuts, raisins, rice bran, millet flakes and apricots or dates.

Store in an airtight container for 1–2 weeks and serve with sliced banana.

Per serving: 389 kcals, 23g fat, 3g saturated fat, 42g carbohydrate, 0.06g sodium, 33mg calcium

Breakfast muesli

This muesli is a wonderful option for breakfast: we absolutely love it with thick organic natural yogurt. It is packed full with goodness and is particularly high in fibre into the bargain! **Makes 10-12 servings**

75g (3oz) hazelnuts
50g (2oz) sunflower seeds
50g (2oz) flaked almonds
50g (2oz) cashew nuts
100g (3½oz) rice bran
60g (2½oz) soft brown sugar

50g (2oz) pumpkin seeds
50g (2oz) raisins
25g (1oz) desiccated coconut
2 tablespoons lecithin (optional)

Preheat the oven to 180°C/350°F/gas mark 4.

Put the hazelnuts on a baking sheet and bake in the oven until the skins start to flake away. Rub off the skins with a clean tea-towel and cut each hazelnut in half.

Place the sunflower seeds on a separate baking sheet and roast in the oven for 5–10 minutes until they are slightly toasted. Repeat this process with the flaked almonds and then the cashew nuts. (Don't be tempted to mix them together as the sunflower seeds, flaked almonds and cashew nuts may not roast in the same length of time.)

Put the rice bran into a large bowl, add the other ingredients and mix well.

Serve with fresh fruit and fresh creamy milk or yogurt. Store muesli in an airtight container – it will keep for 2–3 weeks in a cool place.

Per serving: 260 kcals, 18g fat, 3g saturated fat, 18g carbohydrate, 0.01g sodium, 43mg calcium

Breakfast health bars

There's no substitute for a healthy breakfast, but some people just prefer to do without. These tasty bars are a nutritious option for those on the go – great for a mid-morning snack or a treat in lunchboxes. **Makes 12**

225g (8oz) rice flakes
200ml (7fl oz) apple juice, organic if possible
75g (3oz) butter
40g (1½oz) soft brown sugar
2 eggs, preferably free range
25g (1oz) nibbed almonds
25g (1oz) sunflower seeds

60g (2½oz) ready-to-eat dried figs, chopped
50g (2oz) dates, chopped

Swiss roll tin, 28 x 18cm (11 x 7 in), lined with parchment paper

Preheat the oven to 180°C/350°F/gas mark 4.

Place the rice flakes in a bowl and pour over the apple juice. Leave to soak for at least 1 hour, by which time all the apple juice should be absorbed by the rice flakes.

Cream the butter, and add the sugar. Beat until pale, light and fluffy. In another bowl, whisk the eggs and gradually add to the creamed mixture. Beat together until combined. Fold in the apple-soaked rice flakes, nibbed almonds, sunflower seeds and the chopped figs and dates.

Pour into the lined tin, smooth the surface with a palette knife and bake in the oven for 25 minutes until pale golden. Allow to cool in the tin and cut into 12.

Store in an airtight container and use within a week.

Per bar: 148 kcals, 9g fat, 4g saturated fat, 14g carbohydrate, 0.08g sodium, 32mg calcium

Raspberry muffins

Here's a different muffin, lighter than the classic blueberry one. These teeny-weeny raspberry treats baked in petit four cases are adorable to serve with coffee.

Makes 16 regular muffins or 24 mini muffins

175g (6oz) butter

75g (3oz) ground almonds

1½ tablespoons lemon rind

140g (4½oz) gluten-free icing sugar, sifted, plus extra for dusting (optional)

2 tablespoons fine cornmeal (polenta), sifted

3 tablespoons cornflour, sifted

5 egg whites, preferably free range

175g (6oz) fresh raspberries

Bun tin lined with paper cases

Preheat the oven to 200°C/400°F/gas mark 6.

Melt the butter in a saucepan and cook until it is very light golden in colour.

Mix together the ground almonds, lemon rind, icing sugar cornmeal and cornflour in a large bowl and pour in the melted butter. Gently mix together and fold in the lightly beaten egg whites.

Pour the mixture into the paper cases (or use 24 *petit four* cases to make mini ones) and dot with raspberries.

Bake in the oven for 15 minutes until golden and springy to touch.

Cool on wire racks and sprinkle with extra gluten-free icing sugar, if you wish, before serving.

Per muffin: 99 kcals, 7g fat, 3g saturated fat, 8g carbohydrate, 0.06g sodium, 20mg calcium

Blueberry muffins

The all-American favourite, any time of day. To ring the changes, fresh blackberries, raspberries, loganberries or mulberries can be added instead of blueberries.

Makes 12

175g (6oz) rice flour

50g (2oz) tapioca flour

1 teaspoon bicarbonate of soda

2 teaspoons gluten-free baking powder

1 rounded teaspoon xanthan gum

¼ teaspoon salt

150g (5oz) caster sugar

60g (2½oz) butter, melted and cooled

1 egg, preferably free range, beaten

200ml (7fl oz) buttermilk

150g (5oz) fresh blueberries

12-hole muffin tin lined with paper cases

Preheat the oven to 180°C/350°F/gas mark 4.

Sift together the rice flour, tapioca flour, bicarbonate of soda, baking powder and xanthan gum in a large mixing bowl. Add the salt and sugar and mix well.

Whisk together the cooled melted butter, egg and buttermilk in another large bowl. Make a well in the centre of the dry ingredients and pour in the butter, egg and buttermilk mixture. Stir gently with a wooden spoon to combine and finally gently fold in the blueberries.

Divide the batter equally between the 12 muffin cases and bake in the oven for approximately 25 minutes or until a skewer inserted into the centre comes out cleanly. They are nicest served warm.

Per muffin: 171 kcals, 5g fat, 3g saturated fat, 31g carbohydrate, 0.31g sodium, 42mg calcium

Crumpets

These can be made in minutes with ingredients you probably have in the cupboard. Crumpets are the ideal solution if a friend drops in and there's nothing in the tin. This version has been adapted from a recipe by Florence Bowe. **Makes about 15**

150g (5oz) rice flour
75g (3oz) tapioca flour
1 teaspoon xanthan gum
¼ teaspoon salt
½ teaspoon bicarbonate of soda

1 teaspoon cream of tartar
50g (2oz) caster sugar
25g (1oz) butter
2 eggs, preferably free range
225ml (8fl oz) milk

Sift together the dry ingredients into a bowl and rub in the butter. Drop the eggs into the centre, add a little of the milk and stir rapidly with a whisk allowing the flour to drop gradually in from the sides. When half the milk is added, beat until air bubbles rise. Add the remainder of the milk and allow to stand for 1 hour if possible. (The crumpets are usually lighter if the batter is allowed to stand, but if you need to cook them immediately you'll still get very acceptable results.)

Drop a good dessertspoonful into a hot-ish non-stick frying pan and cook until bubbles appear on the top. It usually takes a bit of trial and error to get the temperature right. Flip over and cook until golden on the other side. Serve immediately with butter and homemade jam or, better still, apple jelly.

Per crumpet: 100 kcals, 3g fat, 1g saturated fat, 17g carbohydrate, 0.25g sodium, 33mg calcium

Ulster fadge or potato bread

Rosemary comes from lovely Derry, so we simply had to include a potato bread – just the thing to bring the light to an Ulsterman's eye! **Makes 10**

40g (1¼oz) butter
1 egg, preferably free range, lightly beaten
700g (1¼lb) hot mashed potatoes
25g (1oz) potato flour

Salt and freshly ground black pepper
Seasoned potato flour, for dusting
Butter or extra virgin olive oil, for frying

Mix the butter and egg together with the hot mashed potatoes. Add the potato flour, salt and freshly ground black pepper to taste. Beat together until the mixture is smooth and lump free.

Allow the mixture to cool and then form into 10 or 12 portions. Sprinkle the work surface with potato flour and, with a rolling pin, carefully form each portion into a square measuring about 10 x 10cm (4 x 4in).

Dip each flattened piece of potato bread into seasoned potato flour and cook by either of the following methods:

Melt a little butter or extra virgin olive oil on a griddle or in a frying pan and add the potato bread. Use the back of a spatula or fish slice to form an indentation across the diagonal of each square of potato bread – being careful not to cut all the way through. Cook over a low heat for about 4–5 minutes on each side so that it is nice and golden and crusty.

Alternatively, preheat the oven to 180°C/350°F/gas mark 4, place each square of potato bread on a baking sheet and make an indentation across the diagonal as before. Place the baking sheet in the oven for 15–20 minutes.

Serve with an Ulster fry (full fried breakfast) or just on its own on hot plates with a blob of butter melting on top.

Per serving: 127 kcals, 7g fat, 4g saturated fat, 14g carbohydrate, 0.29g sodium, 10mg calcium

American buttermilk pancakes

Maple syrup and crispy bacon are the classic accompaniment but cream cheese with smoked salmon, mackerel or spicy sausages are also delicious. **Makes 14–15 x 7cm (3in) pancakes**

175ml (6fl oz) buttermilk
1 egg, preferably free range
15g (½oz) butter, melted
50g (2oz) tapioca flour
25g (1oz) fine cornmeal
Good pinch of salt

1 teaspoon bicarbonate
  of soda
Clarified butter (see page 112)
To serve
Crispy bacon
Maple syrup

Mix the buttermilk, egg and melted butter in a large bowl, until smooth and blended. Sift together the tapioca flour, fine cornmeal, salt and bicarbonate of soda and gently stir into the buttermilk only until the ingredients are moistened – don't worry about the lumps.

Heat a heavy iron or non-stick pan until medium hot. Grease with a little clarified butter. Spoon 1 generous tablespoon of batter onto the pan and spread slightly with the back of the spoon.

Cook until the bubbles rise and break on the top of the pancake. Flip over gently. Cook until pale golden on the other side. Remove and keep warm. Continue until all the batter has been used.

Spread each pancake with butter and serve a stack of three per person with crispy bacon and maple syrup.

Per pancake: 38 kcals, 2g fat, 1g saturated fat, 5g carbohydrate, 0.18g sodium, 18mg calcium

Kedgeree

This immediately conjures up images of country-house breakfasts which were often a veritable feast. This is a very decadent version; if you want to be more frugal, omit the butter and cream – but that would be a shame. **Serves 6–8**

450g (1lb) wild or organic salmon, freshly cooked, or 225g (8oz) salmon and 225g (8oz) cooked smoked haddock or smoked mackerel
225g (8oz) long-grain rice
3 eggs, preferably free range
150ml (5fl oz) single cream
40g (1½oz) butter
3 tablespoons chopped parsley
1½ tablespoons chopped chives
Salt and freshly ground black pepper
Pinch of cayenne pepper

If using salmon, poach the piece of salmon in a small pan just large enough to fit it, cover with boiling salted water (use 1 dessertspoon salt to every 600ml (1 pint) water. Bring to the boil, cover and simmer for just 20 minutes. Turn off the heat, cover and leave to sit for a few minutes before removing from the water. Allow to cool.

Meanwhile, cook the rice in boiling salted water for about 8–10 minutes, then drain. Hard-boil the eggs in boiling salted water for 10 minutes. Drain, and cool immediately under cold running water. Peel and roughly chop.

Remove the skin and any bones from the fish and flake into small pieces.

Heat the cream and butter in a saucepan and add the parsley and chives. As soon as it bubbles, add the rice, flaked fish and the hard-boiled eggs, and season well with salt, freshly ground pepper and a pinch of cayenne. Mix very gently. Taste and adjust the seasoning if necessary, pile into a hot dish and serve with freshly baked gluten-free bread or with hot buttered gluten-free toast.

Per serving: 420 kcals, 23g fat, 9g saturated fat, 34g carbohydrate, 0.15g sodium, 64mg calcium

Hash browns with crispy bacon

A really tasty treat to make for brunch. They are also delicious served with some slivers of good-quality smoked salmon, preferably organic, and a sprinkling of chives. **Serves 4**

450g (1lb) potatoes, peeled
Salt and freshly ground black pepper
150g (5oz) onions, peeled
2 eggs, preferably free range, beaten
1 tablespoon potato flour
1 tablespoon chopped chives
75g (3oz) mature Cheddar cheese
4–6 tablespoons olive oil
8 hot crispy rashers of bacon
Flat parsley, to garnish

Using the coarse side of a grater, grate the potatoes and onions. Place in a colander and sprinkle with a little salt. Allow to drain for 30 minutes. After this time, squeeze out any excess liquid from the potato and onion mixture and pat dry with kitchen paper.

Lightly beat the eggs in a glass bowl. Stir in the potato flour, chopped chives and grated cheese. Add the grated potato and onion and mix well together until combined. Season with salt and freshly ground black pepper.

Heat a little olive oil in a heavy-based non-stick frying pan and cook a small amount of the mixture. Taste for seasoning and adjust if necessary. When you are satisfied with the flavour, heat a couple more tablespoons of oil in the pan and place a tablespoon of the mixture in the hot oil. Flatten slightly with the back of a spoon and cook until golden brown, before flipping it over to cook the other side. Continue to cook the remainder of the mixture in this way, being careful not to overcrowd the pan.

These hash browns may be kept warm if placed uncovered in a low oven for up to 30 minutes.

Place two hash browns per person on hot plates and top with a couple of rashers of hot crispy bacon. Garnish with a sprig of flat parsley and serve immediately.

Per serving: 466 kcals, 29g fat, 10g saturated fat, 28g carbohydrate, 1.36g sodium, 175mg calcium

Congee with chicken, shrimps and mushrooms

Congee is rice porridge – a staple breakfast food in China, often eaten with doughsticks to dunk. We love it as a soup, varying the additions. **Serves 4–6**

225g (8oz) jasmine rice, well-washed and drained
2 litres (3½ pints) water
100g (3½oz) shrimps
100g (3½oz) shredded raw chicken breast
1 teaspoon ginger, grated
1 chilli, thinly sliced (optional)
100g (3½oz) mushrooms, thinly sliced
a little vegetable oil
Salt and freshly ground black pepper
1–2 tablespoons sesame oil
2 tablespoons spring onions, thinly sliced at an angle
2 tablespoons coriander leaves

Put the rice into a saucepan, cover with water, bring to the boil, cover and simmer for 30–40 minutes or until it is cooked and slightly soupy. Add the shrimps, finely shredded chicken, ginger and chilli to the rice, and cook for 4–5 minutes.

Meanwhile sauté the mushrooms in a hot frying pan in a very little oil. Season with salt and freshly ground black pepper. Add to the soup, drizzle with sesame oil and sprinkle with spring onion and coriander leaves. Taste and correct the seasoning if necessary.

Per serving: 293 kcals, 4g fat, 1g saturated fat, 49g carbohydrate, 1.08g sodium, 91mg calcium

Porridge

The Scots know a good nourishing thing when they see one: porridge has long been sustaining the nation through cold winters. Here's the great gluten-free way to start the day!
Serves 2

40g (1½oz) brown rice flakes
Pinch of salt
250ml (9fl oz) milk
2 teaspoons rice bran
15g (½oz) butter

To serve
Single cream or milk
Soft brown sugar

Place the rice flakes in a sieve and allow cold water to run through and rinse them. Put the washed rice flakes into a bowl and cover with cold water. Leave to soak for 3–4 minutes. Drain well.

Place the soaked rice flakes in a small saucepan, add the salt, milk, rice bran and a knob of butter. Simmer gently for 5 minutes, stirring occasionally.

Serve with single cream or milk and soft brown sugar melting over the top.

Per serving: 161 kcals, 10g fat, 6g saturated fat, 12g carbohydrate, 0.35g sodium, 171mg calcium

2

Soups and Salads

Moro's chilled almond soup with grapes and sherry vinegar

Sam Clarke, from the famous Moro restaurant in London, showed us how to make this soup. This is our gluten-free version of it! **Serves 4**

225g (8oz) whole blanched almonds, preferably Spanish
700ml (1¼ pints) iced water
75g (3oz) stale gluten-free white bread (see page 118), crusts removed
3 garlic cloves
1 teaspoon sea salt
3 tablespoons sherry vinegar
3 tablespoons olive oil
225g (8oz) white grapes, preferably Muscat, halved

Grind the almonds in a food processor until the consistency is as fine as possible. (Grinding the almonds for a long time, so that they become moist and warm, causes an amazing marzipan taste to develop which makes this soup so special.) At this point they should stick to the side of the machine. Turn off the machine and loosen the nuts from around the edge and add 5 tablespoons of the ice-cold water. Turn on the machine and the almonds should form a paste-like 'ball' just fluid enough to be able to turn in on itself when the machine is running. Now add the gluten-free bread, and a little more of the ice-cold water to make a smooth, runny liquid. Continue to process for a further minute.

Crush the garlic to a paste with the sea salt and add to the contents of the food processor, along with the sherry vinegar. Combine until smooth. Add the olive oil and gradually pour in the rest of the iced water, until you end up with a nice balance between the almonds, garlic and sherry vinegar. Chill the soup for at least 1 hour. (Alternatively, if you want to make this soup a day in advance, only add the garlic and oil on the day you are going to serve it.) Taste, and adjust the seasoning if necessary.

Ladle into bowls and distribute the grapes evenly. Drizzle with a little extra olive oil if desired. This soup is perfect for a fine summer's day.

Per serving: 534 kcals, 44g fat, 4g saturated fat, 21g carbohydrate, 0.08g sodium, 168mg calcium

Chicken and garlic soup

Don't be put off by the amount of garlic used in this soup. In fact it is deliciously mild with really subtle hints of garlic. The addition of egg yolks and olive oil gives it a sublime texture. **Serves 6–8**

2 large heads of garlic, the unpeeled cloves separated and smashed
1.8 litres (3 pints) homemade light chicken stock (see page 153) or water
2 teaspoons salt
Large pinch of freshly ground white pepper
2 whole cloves
¼ teaspoon chopped sage
¼ teaspoon chopped thyme
1 medium bay leaf
6 parsley sprigs
3 tablespoons fruity olive oil
2 skinless and boneless chicken breasts, preferably free range
For the final liaison
3 egg yolks, preferably free range
50ml (2fl oz) olive oil
2–3 tablespoons chopped parsley

Combine all the soup ingredients, except the chicken, in a large saucepan. Bring to the boil and simmer, partially covered, for 30 minutes. Strain into a bowl, pressing the juices out of the ingredients and return the liquid to the saucepan. Taste and adjust the seasoning if necessary.

While the soup base is simmering, cut the chicken breasts into 1cm (½in) dice, or julienne. Add the chicken to the soup base and allow to simmer for 4–5 minutes.

Whisk the egg yolks in a mixing bowl for 1–2 minutes until thick and sticky, then whisk in the olive oil drop by drop to make a thick, mayonnaise-like cream. Just before serving, whisk the soup into the liaison and fold in the parsley. Serve immediately with homemade gluten-free bread.

Per serving: 224 kcals, 17g fat, 3g saturated fat, 2g carbohydrate, 1.08g sodium, 67mg calcium

French onion soup with gruyère croûtons

A fragrant and warming soup that is traditionally served with cheese croûtons. You could use parmesan instead of, or together with gruyère, if you like. **Serves 6**

50g (2oz) butter
1.3kg (3lb) onions, thinly sliced
1.8 litres (3 pints) homemade beef, chicken or vegetable stock (see pages 152–153)
Salt and freshly ground black pepper

To finish
6 slices gluten-free white bread (see page 118), 1cm (½in) thick, toasted
75g (3oz) Gruyère cheese, grated

Melt the butter in a saucepan. Add the onions and cook over a low heat for about 40–60 minutes with the lid off, stirring frequently – the onions should be dark and well caramelised but not burnt. Hold your nerve: the onions must be very well caramelised, otherwise the soup will be too weak and sweet. Add the stock, season with salt and freshly ground black pepper, bring to the boil and cook for a further 10 minutes.

Meanwhile, place the toasted slices of gluten-free bread on a chopping board and cut 6 circles out of the bread using a plain 8cm (3½in) pastry cutter. Cover each toasted circle with grated cheese. Preheat the grill.

Ladle the soup into deep soup bowls or tureens, and put a cheese-topped croûton on top of each one. Pop the bowls under the hot grill until the cheese melts and turns golden brown. Serve immediately, but beware – it will be very hot. Bon appetit!

Per serving: 287 kcals, 13g fat, 8g saturated fat, 34g carbohydrate, 0.78g sodium, 252mg calcium

Mushroom soup

This is one of the easiest soups of all to make. Choose flat mushrooms or button mushrooms that are a few days old, which have developed a slightly stronger flavour and use potato flour to thicken. **Serves 8–9**

450g (1lb) mushrooms
110g (4oz) onions
25g (1oz) butter
600ml (1 pint) homemade
   chicken or vegetable stock
   (see pages 152–153)

600ml (1 pint) milk
25g (1oz) potato flour
Salt and freshly ground black
   pepper
Dash of single cream
   (optional)

Rinse the mushrooms quickly under cold running water. Chop the onions finely. Melt the butter in a saucepan on a gentle heat. Toss the onions in the butter. Cover and sweat until soft and completely cooked.

Meanwhile, chop the mushrooms very finely. Add to the pan and cook on a high heat for 4–5 minutes. (Alternatively, just slice and then whiz in a liquidiser for a few seconds when the soup is cooked. The stalks may also be used.)

Bring the stock and milk to the boil in a separate pan. Stir the potato flour into the onions and cook on a low heat for 2–3 minutes. Season with salt and freshly ground black pepper, then add the stock and milk gradually, stirring all the time. Increase the heat and bring to the boil. Taste and add a dash of cream if necessary. Serve immediately or cool and reheat later. Mushroom soup freezes perfectly.

Per serving: 84 kcals, 4g fat, 2g saturated fat, 8g carbohydrate, 0.26g sodium, 109mg calcium

Autumn vegetable and rice soup

A delicious chunky soup with lots of vegetables. Up to 225g (8oz) cooked haricot beans or black-eyed beans can be added instead of rice for an even more robust and gutsy soup. **Serves 8**

50g (2oz) butter
110g (4oz) onions, finely
   chopped
110g (4oz) carrots, cut into
   5mm (¼in) dice
110g (4oz) celery, cut into
   5mm (¼in) dice
Salt and freshly ground black
   pepper
110g (4oz) parsnips, cut into
   5mm (¼in) dice
110g (4oz) turnips, cut into
   5mm (¼in) dice
175g (6oz) potatoes, peeled

and cut into 5mm (¼in) dice
110g (4oz) leeks, cut into
   5mm (¼in) slices
450g (1lb) very ripe tomatoes,
   peeled and diced, or 400ml
   (14fl oz) tinned tomatoes,
   and their juice, chopped
Pinch of sugar
1.8 litres (3 pints) homemade
   chicken or vegetable stock
   (see pages 152–153)
75g (3oz) Basmati rice
Chopped flat parsley,
   to garnish

Melt the butter on a low heat in a large, heavy-based saucepan, add the onions, carrots and celery. (Use a vegetable peeler to remove the strings from the celery, otherwise they will catch in your teeth.) Season with salt and freshly ground black pepper and sweat for 5 minutes.

Add the parsnips, turnips, potatoes and leeks and sweat for a further 5 minutes. Add the chopped tomatoes with a pinch of sugar and bring to the boil. Add the stock and, once it has come back to the boil, stir in the Basmati rice. Reduce the heat and simmer for about 8–9 minutes, or until the rice is just cooked. Taste and adjust the seasoning if necessary.

Serve scattered with parsley.

Per serving: 138 kcals, 6g fat, 3g saturated fat, 19g carbohydrate, 0.5g sodium, 72mg calcium

Minestrone

Now coeliacs can enjoy this famous Italian soup. Make a big batch and freeze in clean plastic containers for a later date, with the minimum of effort. A drizzle of pesto (page 148) over each bowl makes it even more irresistible. **Serves 10**

110g (4oz) dried haricot beans, soaked overnight in plenty of cold water

1 bouquet garni, consisting of a parsley stalk, a sprig of thyme and a bay leaf tied together with a piece of string

50g (2oz) rindless streaky bacon, cut into 1cm (½in) dice

4 tablespoons olive oil

110g (4oz) onions, finely chopped

110g (4oz) carrots, cut into 5mm (¼in) dice

110g (4oz) celery, cut into 5mm (¼in) dice

Salt and freshly ground black pepper

450g (1lb) very ripe tomatoes, peeled and diced, or 400ml (14fl oz) tinned tomatoes, and their juice, chopped

Pinch of sugar

1 garlic clove, crushed

2 litres (3½ pints) homemade chicken or vegetable stock (see pages 152–3)

1 bay leaf

110g (4oz) leeks, cut into 5mm (¼in) slices

110g (4oz) green beans, sliced at an angle into 3

1 small cauliflower, divided into small florets

75g (3oz) gluten-free small macaroni

2 medium courgettes, green or golden, cut into 1cm (½in) dice, or 225g (8oz) Savoy cabbage, shredded

Chopped parsley

To serve

110g (4oz) Parmesan, freshly grated

Drain the soaked haricot beans and place in a saucepan. Cover with fresh cold water and add the bouquet garni. Cover the pan and simmer until the beans are soft but not mushy – this can take 30–60 minutes. Drain the cooked beans and discard the bouquet garni but reserve the cooking liquid.

Blanch the bacon in cold water to remove some of the salt, drain and dry on kitchen paper.

Heat the olive oil on a gentle heat in a large, heavy-based pan, add the bacon and sauté over a medium heat for 1–2 minutes until crisp and golden. Remove to a plate and toss the onions, carrots and celery into the oil and bacon fat. Season with salt and freshly ground black pepper and sauté for 5 minutes or until lightly browned. Add the chopped fresh or tinned tomatoes and a pinch of sugar. Stir in the crushed garlic, and simmer over a low heat for 5 minutes.

Add the stock and bay leaf and bring to the boil. Add the leeks and green beans.

Cover and simmer on a gentle heat for 5 minutes. Add the cauliflower florets and gluten-free macaroni and continue to cook until the pasta is *al dente*.

Add the courgettes or cabbage and crispy bacon and simmer for a further 5 minutes. Remove the bay leaf and add the chopped parsley. Add the cooked haricot beans to the saucepan and 600ml (1 pint) of the reserved cooking liquid. Return to the boil and simmer until the haricot beans are heated through. Taste and adjust the seasoning if necessary.

Serve immediately in warm bowls with freshly grated Parmesan sprinkled on top.

Per serving: 160 kcals, 7g fat, 1g saturated fat, 18g carbohydrate, 0.48g sodium, 89mg calcium

Warm salad of sesame-crusted chicken with avocado and pancetta

This makes a really tasty starter or a lunch. Toss the ingredients together at the last minute. **Serves 4**

2 chicken breasts, preferably free range

Sea salt and freshly ground pepper

4 tablespoons sesame seeds

3 tablespoons extra virgin olive oil

175g (6oz) baby spinach leaves

1 perfectly ripe avocado

1 tablespoon sunflower oil

100g (3½oz) gluten-free pancetta, cut into 1cm (½in) cubes

Parmesan

For the dressing

2 tablespoons freshly squeezed lemon juice

4 tablespoons extra virgin olive oil

½ teaspoon gluten-free Dijon mustard

Cut the chicken breasts into 1 cm (½in) strips at an angle and season. Put the sesame seeds on a large plate and mix with a good pinch of sea salt and freshly ground black pepper. Dip the chicken strips first into the olive oil and then into the sesame seeds to coat them on both sides. Place the sesame-coated chicken strips on a sheet of parchment paper and refrigerate until required.

Make the salad dressing by whisking all the ingredients together in a small bowl. Season to taste.

Wash the baby spinach and use a salad-spinner to dry the leaves. Put them into a large bowl. Peel the avocado, halve and remove the stone. Cut each half into slices 1cm (½in) wide. Add the avocado slices to the spinach.

Heat two frying pans to a medium temperature. When they are hot, add the sunflower oil to one and then add the sesame chicken strips. Allow the sesame seeds to become golden on one side before turning over so that they develop a gorgeous nutty flavour. Do not agitate the pan too much or you will lose the sesame seeds. Add the pancetta cubes to the second pan and cook them until they are golden and crispy.

As soon as the chicken and pancetta are ready, toss them with the spinach and avocado in the bowl. Pour over the dressing and toss everything together quickly so that the leaves glisten with the dressing. Pile the salad high onto a serving dish or individual plates.

Using a potato peeler, shave long strips of Parmesan over the top of the salad and serve immediately.

Per serving: 541 kcals, 47g fat, 9g saturated fat, 2g carbohydrate, 0.6g sodium, 225mg calcium

Thai rice noodle salad
This light and delicious salad can of course be served on its own but we love it with Thai Fishcakes (see page 95). **Serves 4–6**

225g (8oz) gluten-free fine rice noodles (vermicelli or cellophane)
8 spring onions
1 red pepper
110–175g (4–6oz) mangetout
50g (2oz) red-skin peanuts, (optional)
Chopped coriander
Salt and freshly ground black pepper

For the dressing
4 tablespoons sesame oil
2 red chillies, finely chopped
3 garlic cloves, crushed
5cm (2in) fresh ginger, grated
1 tablespoon white wine vinegar
1 tablespoon gluten-free nam pla (fish sauce)
2 tablespoons gluten-free Japanese tamari soy sauce
1 teaspoon sugar

Soak the rice noodles in boiling water for about 4 minutes until soft. Drain them through a colander and place on kitchen paper.

Meanwhile make the dressing. Heat 3 tablespoons of the sesame oil in a pan and cook the chillies, garlic and ginger for 3 minutes until slightly softened. Leave to cool, then add the remaining dressing ingredients.

Preheat the oven to 180°C/350°F/gas mark 4, if using the peanuts. Place them on a baking sheet and roast for about 8 minutes. Rub off the skins using a clean tea towel and chop.

Prepare the vegetables. Thinly slice the spring onions at an angle. Quarter and core the red pepper and cut into fine strips at an angle. Blanch the mangetout in a pot of boiling water (2 teaspoons salt to 1.2 litres (2 pints) water) for 1 minute. Drain and refresh under cold running water. Slice in half at an angle.

Mix the dressing through the drained noodles, then add the vegetables and roasted peanuts (if using). Add the chopped coriander. Taste for seasoning and adjust if necessary.

Per serving: 343 kcals, 11g fat, 2g saturated fat, 58g carbohydrate, 0.91g sodium, 37mg calcium

Vietnamese noodle salad
A delicious light and fresh-tasting salad. Serve as a starter or as an accompaniment to Crispy Basil and Pine Nut Chicken Sandwich (see page 97). **Serves 4**

200g (7oz) gluten-free flat rice noodles
Fresh coriander leaves
20g (¾oz) freshly roasted peanuts (optional)

For the dressing
4 tablespoons gluten-free nam pla (fish sauce)
2 tablespoons fresh lime juice
1–2 red chillies, finely chopped
1 garlic clove, crushed
1 tablespoon soft brown sugar
3 spring onions, finely sliced at an angle

Combine all the ingredients for the dressing together in a bowl and stir until the sugar is dissolved.

Just before serving bring a kettle of water to the boil. Place the flat rice noodles in a large bowl and pour over the boiling water. The noodles should be completely covered. Allow to soak for about 6 minutes or until softened.

Drain thoroughly through a colander and return to the bowl. Pour over the dressing and toss the noodles well to ensure they are all coated with the dressing.

Sprinkle with coriander leaves and roasted chopped peanuts (if using) and serve immediately.

Per serving: 190 kcals, 0g fat, 0g saturated fat, 46g carbohydrate, 1.08g sodium, 23mg calcium

Salade tiède with prawns and green beans and a lemon and dill dressing

Salades tièdes or warm salads are a combination of lettuce, salad and herb leaves with a few tasty hot delicacies. **Serves 4**

A selection of lettuces, herbs and salad leaves, e.g. butterhead, frisée, oakleaf, watercress, rocket, salad burnet, golden marjoram
20 large very fresh raw prawns (e.g. Dublin Bay prawns)
Salt
275g (10oz) baby new potatoes, well scrubbed
225g (8oz) French beans
75–125ml (3–4fl oz) gluten-free French dressing
8 spring onions, finely sliced at an angle
Cracked black pepper

For the dressing
4 tablespoons crème fraîche (see page 64)
1–2 tablespoons freshly squeezed lemon juice
1 tablespoon finely chopped dill

Wash and dry the salad leaves, and tear the larger ones into bite-sized pieces.

Now prepare the prawns. Remove the head and discard. With the underside of each prawn uppermost, tug the little fan-shaped tail at either side and carefully draw out the black vein (the trail is the intestine, so it is very important to remove it before cooking).

Bring 3.5 litres (6 pints) water to the boil and add 3 tablespoons of salt. Put the prawns into the fast-boiling salted water. As soon as the water returns to the boil, test a prawn to see if it is cooked. A cooked prawn should be firm and white, not opaque or mushy; it should also rise to the top. When they are cooked, remove the prawns from the water immediately. Very large ones may take 30 seconds–1 minute more.

Leave the prawns to cool on a tray in a single layer, then remove the shells.

While the prawns are cooling, cook the potatoes in boiling salted water for approximately 10 minutes, until just tender.

Top and tail the French beans and cut in half at an angle. Bring 1.2 litres (2 pints) water to a fast rolling boil, add 2 teaspoons salt and then toss in the beans. Continue to boil very fast for 5–6 minutes or until just cooked (they should still retain a little bite). Drain immediately.

Make the lemon and dill dressing by whisking all the ingredients together in a small bowl.

When the potatoes are ready, drain well and cut them into quarters. Toss the potatoes with the French beans in a little of the gluten-free French dressing so that they absorb all the flavours while warm.

Meanwhile, toss the salad leaves lightly in just enough lemon and dill dressing to make the leaves glisten. Divide the salad leaves between 4 warm plates, piling them up in the centre. Arrange the warm dressed potatoes and French beans around the salad and scatter each plate with 5 prawns. Drizzle each one with the lemon and dill dressing. Sprinkle with the finely sliced spring onions and a little freshly cracked black pepper. Serve immediately.

Per serving: 202 kcals, 7g fat, 4g saturated fat, 14g carbohydrate, 0.35g sodium, 129mg calcium

Roast wild salmon, cherry tomato and asparagus salad

The season for wild salmon is short, but if you can source it for this colourful salad, it tastes sublime. Otherwise, try to buy organic farmed salmon. **Serves 4–6**

450g (1lb) wild (or organic) salmon

Sea salt and freshly ground black pepper

Extra virgin olive oil

1 small red onion, thinly sliced into half moons

2 garlic cloves, crushed

2 teaspoons grated ginger

1 teaspoon freshly roasted and crushed cumin seeds

½ teaspoon ground turmeric

400g (14oz) tinned chickpeas

12 asparagus spears

12–18 cherry tomatoes, halved

½ cucumber, cut in half lengthwise and then sliced

2 tablespoons chopped mint

Selection of salad leaves

For the dressing

6 tablespoons virgin olive oil

2 tablespoons white wine vinegar

Sugar

Preheat the oven to 230°C/450°F/gas mark 8.

Line a baking tray with aluminium foil and put the salmon on top, skin-side down. Season with salt and pepper and and drizzle with oil. Cook in the oven for about 10 minutes or until just cooked but still a little pink in the centre.

Heat 2 tablespoons oil in a sauté pan, and add the onion, garlic and ginger. Cook, stirring, for 3–4 minutes, then add the cumin and turmeric and cook for a further minute or two. Rinse the chickpeas under cold running water, drain well, add to the pan and cook for 4–5 minutes. Season to taste and cool.

Trim the root end of the asparagus and peel if you wish. Toss the spears in oil, sprinkle with sea salt and roast in the oven for 5 minutes.

Whisk together the dressing ingredients, season and sprinkle over the tomatoes and cucumber in a small bowl. Add the mint and toss gently. Just before serving, toss the salad leaves with a little dressing. Mix the chickpeas with the tomatoes and cucumber, then pile on top of the salad.

Flake the salmon into large pieces and scatter over the top, interspersed with the roasted asparagus spears cut at an angle.

Per serving: 489 kcals, 33g fat, 5g saturated fat, 17g carbohydrate, 0.35g sodium, 116mg calcium

Panzanella

Several countries, especially around the Mediterranean, have devised delicious ways of using up bread: this one originates from the gorgeous region of Tuscany in Italy. Substitute marjoram for basil if you prefer. **Serves 6**

110g (4oz) gluten-free white bread (see page 118)

3–4 tablespoons extra virgin olive oil

Sea salt and freshly ground black pepper

½–1 cucumber

1 red onion

4–6 spring onions, green and white parts

4 vine-ripened tomatoes

12–18 Kalamata olives

2–3 tablespoons chopped parsley

Large bunch of basil, leaves torn

For the dressing

3 tablespoons freshly squeezed lemon juice

6 tablespoons olive oil

2 garlic cloves, crushed

Dash of balsamic vinegar

Preheat the oven to 180°C/350°F/gas mark 4.

Cut the bread into even-sized strips, about 1.5cm (¾in) wide and 5cm (2in) long. Place them in a bowl and drizzle with the olive oil. Toss the strips around, so that they are evenly coated with the oil. Lay on a baking sheet in a single layer, season with sea salt and pepper and bake in the oven for approximately 10–15 minutes or until golden and crispy. Watch them carefully as they may cook unevenly around the edges.

Make the dressing by whisking together all the ingredients. Season to taste.

Halve the cucumber lengthwise and cut it into chunks. Slice the red onion thinly into half-moons. Coarsely chop the spring onions. Core the tomatoes and cut into wedges. Mix the tomatoes, cucumber, onion, spring onions, olives, chopped parsley and torn basil in a bowl with the crispy bread strips. Season with salt and freshly ground black pepper.

Spoon the dressing over the salad, toss gently, taste and adjust the seasoning if necessary. Allow the salad to sit for at least 30 minutes, better still 1 hour, before serving, so that the bread soaks up lots of the yummy dressing and juices.

Per serving: 204 kcals, 17g fat, 2g saturated fat, 12g carbohydrate, 0.39g sodium, 47mg calcium

Feta and watermelon salad

Feta is a Greek ewe's milk cheese, with a salty tang and crumbly texture. Here it is used to made a quick and tasty summery salad. We also make it with Knockalara, an Irish farmhouse cheese. **Serves 4**

- 2–3 tablespoons extra virgin olive oil
- 225g (8oz) feta cheese, cut into 2.5cm (1in) cubes
- ¼ ripe watermelon, cut into 2.5cm (1in) cubes
- 1–2 tablespoons freshly squeezed lemon juice
- Salt and freshly ground black pepper
- 2 tablespoons coarsely snipped flat parsley or spearmint

Drizzle a little of the extra virgin olive oil over the feta cheese. Set aside.

Just before serving, gently toss the watermelon and feta cubes together and sprinkle with the rest of the olive oil and the lemon juice. Season with salt and black pepper.

Transfer to a wide serving dish and scatter with the coarsely snipped parsley or spearmint. Best eaten immediately!

Per serving: 239 kcals, 18g fat, 9g saturated fat, 8g carbohydrate, 1g sodium, 238mg calcium

Roasted red pepper pasta salad with feta cheese

A really tasty and attractive salad that is great in the summer for barbecues. Ideally, select Italian or Spanish red peppers for their superior flavour. **Serves 8–10**

- 1 tablespoon sunflower oil
- 3 red peppers
- 4 tablespoons pesto (see page 148)
- 175ml (6fl oz) gluten-free French dressing
- 225g (8oz) gluten-free penne
- 75g (3oz) pine nuts
- 200g (7oz) feta cheese, cut into 2.5cm (1in) cubes
- 110g (4oz) sun-dried tomatoes (see page 155)
- 6 spring onions
- 3–4 tablespoons annual marjoram, chopped
- Salt and freshly ground black pepper
- 50g (2oz) tiny Tunisian black olives, stoned and chopped

Preheat the oven to 250°C/475°F/gas mark 9.

Rub a little oil over the uncut peppers. Place on a baking sheet and roast for 20–30 minutes. Put them in a bowl, cover with clingfilm and leave until cool enough to handle. Peel, deseed but do not wash. Cut into strips 1.5cm (¾in) wide and set aside. Reduce the oven to 180°C/350°F/gas mark 4.

Whisk the pesto into the French dressing and set aside.

Bring 4.5 litres (8 pints) water to a rolling boil in a large pan and add 1–2 tablespoons salt. Tip the penne in all at once and stir well to ensure the shapes remain separate. Cover the pan just long enough to bring the water back to the boil and cook, uncovered, until *al dente*. Drain, and while the pasta is still while, toss in a little dressing so that it absorbs the flavours.

When the oven temperature has dropped, place the pine nuts on a baking sheet and toast in the oven for 5–10 minutes or until they are slightly golden. Watch carefully as they can burn very easily around the edges. Leave to cool.

Drizzle the cheese with the dressing. Quarter the sun-dried tomatoes and finely slice the spring onions at an angle.

Mix all the ingredients, except the olives, in a bowl with the marjoram. Season to taste. Pour over the rest of the dressing and sprinkle with the olives.

Per serving: 431 kcals, 30g fat, 7g saturated fat, 32g carbohydrate, 0.86g sodium, 158mg calcium

3

Starters

Rice paper spring rolls with thai dipping sauce

Vary the filling as you like. Prawns add sweetness; herbs add freshness. Serve as a starter, main course, or as mini ones with drinks. **Makes 20–40, depending on size**

10g (½oz) gluten-free cellophane or thin rice noodles

110g (4oz) lean pork, minced

110g (4oz) cooked white crab meat, shredded

½–1 teaspoon ginger, freshly grated

1 lemongrass stalk, finely chopped (optional)

110g (4oz) mushrooms, finely chopped

3 spring onions or 40g (1½oz) onions, finely chopped

1 egg, preferably free range, lightly beaten

¼ teaspoon salt

Freshly ground black pepper

Vietnamese rice paper wrappers (15.5cm/6½in diameter for starters, 23cm/9in for a main course portion)

Oil, for deep-frying

To serve

Large soft lettuce (we use butter head)

Bunch of fresh mint

Thai Dipping Sauce (see recipe)

Soak the noodles in a large bowl of hot water (almost too hot to touch) for about 10 minutes or until soft. Drain well and cut into approximately 1cm (½in) lengths.

Put the pork into a bowl with the crab meat, ginger, lemongrass, mushrooms, noodles and finely chopped spring onions or onion. Add the beaten egg. Season with salt and freshly ground black pepper and mix well.

Fill a wide bowl with hot water (almost too hot to handle). Dip a rice paper wrapper in the water for about 8–10 seconds or until it begins to soften. Remove, gently shake off the excess moisture and lay on a clean chopping board.

Put a heaped tablespoon of the mixture roughly a third from the lower edge, but slightly closer to the edge nearest you. Spread the mixture into a sausage shape. Fold the bottom over the filling. Then fold the two sides over to the centre. Roll the parcel away from you and seal.

Make all the spring rolls in the same way and set them aside on a plate.

Heat the oil in a wok or deep-fat fryer to 180°C/350°F or until a cube of day-old gluten-free bread browns in 30 seconds. When the oil is hot, fry a few spring rolls at a time until they are golden. Remove with a slotted spoon and drain on kitchen paper.

Arrange the spring rolls on plates with a few lettuce leaves and mint sprigs (allow 4 or more rolls per person, depending on size). Put a small bowl of dipping sauce on the side.

To eat, take a lettuce leaf, or part of one, and put a spring roll and a few mint sprigs on it; roll it up and dip into the sauce. Alternatively present the spring rolls on a large platter and allow people to help themselves.

Per serving: 184 kcals, 14g fat, 2g saturated fat, 6g carbohydrate, 0.18g sodium, 26mg calcium

Thai dipping sauce
Serves 4

3 tablespoons gluten-free nam pla (fish sauce)

3 tablespoons freshly squeezed lime or lemon juice

3 tablespoons warm water

2 tablespoons sugar, or more to taste

1 garlic clove, crushed

3–4 hot red or green chillies

Put the fish sauce, lime or lemon juice, warm water and sugar into a jar and add the crushed garlic. Mix well and pour into 4 individual bowls. Cut the chillies crosswise into very thin rounds and divide them between the bowls. Taste and balance sweet with sour, salty with sharp.

Per serving: 39 kcals, 0g fat, 0g saturated fat, 9g carbohydrate, 0.8g sodium, 11mg calcium

Vietnamese rice paper rolls with shrimps and fresh herbs

These fresh-tasting spring rolls are all the rage. Feel free to vary the filling — sweet crab meat or cooked salmon are also delicious. **Serves 4**

25g (1oz) rice vermicelli

8–12 medium-to-large raw shrimps or prawns

Salt and black pepper

110g (4oz) grated carrot

½ cucumber, peeled and cut into thin strips or shredded

2 spring onions, white part with a little of the green, trimmed and cut into slivers

Sugar, to taste

Rice vinegar, to taste

4 sheets rice paper, 20–25cm (8–10in) in diameter

20 or more fresh mint leaves

8 or more sprigs of coriander

Vietnamese Dipping Sauce (see recipe)

Lettuce leaves (optional)

Soak the noodles in a large bowl of hot water (almost too hot to touch) for about 10 minutes or until soft. Drain well.

Meanwhile, prepare the other ingredients. Cook the shrimps or prawns in well-salted water until pink (allow 1 tablespoon salt to 1.2 litres (2 pints) water). Cool, then peel and cut each into 2 slices. Season the carrot, cucumber and spring onion with salt, pepper, sugar and a dash of rice vinegar. Taste.

Assemble all the ingredients; you'll also need a bowl of hot water and a clean tea-towel. Put a sheet of rice paper into the water for 15–20 seconds, until just soft (don't let it get too soft; it will continue to soften as you work). Lay it on the towel.

Arrange 2 or 3 shrimps in the middle of the rice paper and about a quarter each of the noodles, carrot, cucumber and spring onion. Don't overfill. Top with a little mint and coriander.

Working quickly, start to roll up the rice paper, tuck in the sides and continue to roll, keeping it fairly tight. Roll in a sheet of pure clingfilm, again making it tight. The prepared rolls can be kept in the fridge for several hours.

Trim the ends of each roll with a sharp knife, then cut into 2.5cm (1in) sections, right through the clingfilm. Unwrap each section and place, cut-side up, on a plate. Alternatively the rolls may be left whole or cut in half at a long angle. Serve with lettuce, coriander and a bowl of dipping sauce.

Per serving: 79 kcals, 1g fat, 0g saturated fat, 12g carbohydrate, 0.3g sodium, 57mg calcium

Vietnamese dipping sauce
Serves 4

2 tablespoons freshly squeezed lime juice

2 tablespoons gluten-free nam pla or nuoc mâm (fish sauce)

1 tablespoon water

½ teaspoon fresh grated ginger

1 teaspoon chopped chilli or dried red pepper flakes

2 teaspoons sugar

Mix together all the ingredients in a small bowl and stir to dissolve the sugar.

Taste and adjust the seasoning if necessary. If time allows, let the sauce sit for 15–30 minutes before serving to allow the flavours to develop. Serve warm or at room temperature.

Per serving: 15 kcals, 0g fat, 0g saturated fat, 3g carbohydrate, 0.53g sodium, 6mg calcium

Courgette and feta fritters
These make a good starter or a light summery lunch. A mixture of green and golden courgettes is particularly delicious. Try basil or marjoram instead of mint occasionally. **Serves 6**

500g (1lb 2oz) courgettes, coarsely grated

½ teaspoon salt

2 eggs, preferably free range, lightly beaten

8 spring onions, finely sliced at an angle

110g (4oz) feta cheese, crumbled

1½ tablespoons fresh chopped mint

60g (2½oz) rice flour

Salt and freshly ground black pepper

Olive oil, for frying

Place the grated courgettes in a colander, sprinkle with salt and allow to degorge for at least 30 minutes. Squeeze out any excess liquid and pat dry with kitchen paper. (You may be surprised at how much liquid will come out.)

Whisk the eggs in a bowl and add the drained courgettes, finely sliced spring onions, crumbled feta and chopped mint. Stir gently so they are well combined. Stir in the rice flour and season with salt and freshly ground black pepper.

Heat a layer of about 1cm (½in) of olive oil in a frying pan and when it is hot gently drop in about a teaspoon of the fritter mixture to check the seasoning. When it is crispy, taste and adjust the seasoning if necessary.

Drop generous tablespoonfuls of the batter into the hot oil, flatten slightly with the back of the spoon, and cook in batches for about 2 minutes on each side until golden brown and crispy.

Remove the cooked fritters with a slotted spoon and drain on kitchen paper. Keep them warm in a low oven (150°C/300°F gas mark 2), but do not cover or they will go soggy. Meanwhile, cook the remainder.

Serve the fritters with a Greek green salad and tsatsiki (see page 154). A little tomato salad would also be very nice.

Per serving: 253 kcals, 20g fat, 5g saturated fat, 10g carbohydrate, 0.49g sodium, 117mg calcium

Tempura
Japanese chefs pride themselves on their light, crispy tempura batter which they use to coat all manner of tasty morsels. Cauliflower florets, mushrooms or spring onions are delicious options. **Serves 4–6**

12 prawns, shelled but with tails still on

Oil, for deep frying

1 courgette, cut into batons

1 small aubergine, cut into slices, 1cm (½in) thick

4 okra (optional)

For the batter

4 tablespoons rice flour

1 tablespoon cornflour

½ teaspoon gluten-free baking powder

700ml (1¼ pints) ice-cold water

1 large egg white, preferably free-range

Salt

For the dipping sauce

Gluten-free Japanese tamari soy sauce

Daikon radish (if available)

Gluten-free wasabi mustard

Remove the shell from the prawns, devein, drawing out the black vein, but leave the tail intact. Butterfly the prawns, keeping them attached at the tail. Heat the oil in a deep-fat fryer to 180°C/350°F.

Meanwhile, make the batter. Sift the rice flour, cornflour and gluten-free baking powder into a bowl. Add the water and whisk just enough to barely combine; don't over-mix. Whisk the egg white in a separate scrupulously clean bowl and fold into the batter with a little salt.

Dip the prawns and vegetables into the batter one by one. Deep-fry the tempura until crisp and allow them to drain on kitchen paper.

Serve immediately, while hot and crisp. Provide each diner with a bowl of gluten-free Japanese tamari soy sauce with a little chopped daikon and a dab of wasabi.

Per serving: 294 kcals, 19g fat, 2g saturated fat, 18g carbohydrate, 0.71g sodium, 80mg calcium

Crispy prawn and coriander cakes

Feta and Watermelon Salad (see page 57) goes splendidly with these yummy little prawn and coriander cakes.

Makes 18 cakes – serves 6

18 large raw Dublin Bay or tiger prawns

3 egg whites, preferably free range, lightly beaten

6 spring onions, finely sliced at an angle

1 red chilli, deseeded and finely chopped

4 tablespoons fresh chopped coriander

50g (2oz) rice flour

Salt and freshly ground black pepper

Extra virgin olive oil, for frying

Salad leaves

Lemon wedges

Remove the head from the prawns and discard. Devein – with the upper side of the prawns uppermost, tug the little fan-shaped tail at either side and carefully draw out the trail. Peel back the shell and discard.

Slice the prawns in half lengthwise. Whisk the egg whites lightly in a clean bowl and add the spring onions, chopped chilli, coriander, rice flour, salt, freshly ground black pepper and prawns.

Heat about 2 tablespoons of the olive oil in a frying pan over a medium heat. Fry a little of the mixture until crisp, taste and adjust the seasoning if necessary.

Place heaped tablespoons of the mixture in the hot frying pan, flatten slightly with the back of a spoon and cook in batches for 1–2 minutes on each side, so that they are crispy and golden and the prawns are cooked through. Try not to overcrowd the pan.

Serve the prawn cakes with a few mixed salad leaves and lemon wedges or Feta and Watermelon Salad for a tasty summer starter.

Per serving: 141 kcals, 6g fat, 2g saturated fat, 7g carbohydrate, 0.22g sodium, 82mg calcium

Pancake parcels

This is a very versatile way to serve pancakes. Serve one as a starter or three per person with a different filling for a substantial main course. The filling can include meat, fish or just a juicy vegetable filling. **Serves 8**

½ quantity savoury pancake batter (see page 151)

Tomato sauce (use the tomato fondue recipe on page 154 and purée through a mouli-légume to make a smooth sauce)

Suggested fillings

Piperonata (see page 80)

Mushroom à la crème (see page 151)

Tomato fondue (see page 154)

Creamed spinach (see page 75)

Seafood

Prepare the pancakes following the recipe. To assemble the parcels, lay a pancake on a clean worktop. Put 2 tablespoons of filling in the middle, fold in the sides and fold over the ends into a parcel. Repeat with the remainder. If the components are cold, place in a shallow ovenproof dish and reheat in a moderate oven (180°C/350°F/gas mark 4) for 15–20 minutes. **Serve** the pancake parcels with a little tomato sauce.

Per serving: 271 kcals, 11g fat, 5g saturated fat, 41g carbohydrate, 0.25g sodium, 78mg calcium

Buckwheat pancakes with smoked salmon, crème fraîche and crispy capers

Buckwheat is deliciously nutty, rich in minerals and B vitamins and is naturally gluten-free. **Serves 8**

8 buckwheat pancakes (see recipe)

16 thin slices of smoked salmon (about 225g/8oz), preferably organic

8 tablespoons crème fraîche (see recipe)

56 capers, rinsed, drained and fried until crisp in a little hot oil

4 tablespoons finely chopped spring onions or chives, cut at an angle

Freshly ground black pepper

Fold the pancakes on warm serving plates, and divide the smoked salmon between them.

Allow about 1 tablespoon crème fraîche for each pancake. Sprinkle 7 capers and ½ tablespoon chopped spring onions or chives over each serving. Season with freshly ground black pepper and serve immediately.

Per serving: 176 kcals, 11g fat, 6g saturated fat, 9g carbohydrate, 0.9g sodium, 51mg calcium

Buckwheat pancake batter
Makes 12 x 18cm (7in) pancakes

2 tablespoons butter

225ml (8fl oz) milk

1 teaspoon salt

¼ teaspoon sugar

60g (2½oz) rice flour

2½ tablespoons buckwheat flour

1½ teaspoons vegetable oil

2 small eggs, preferably free range

40ml (1½fl oz) sparkling mineral water

Melt the butter in a small pan. Add the milk, salt and sugar, stir well and turn off the heat.

Put both flours in a mixing bowl, make a well in the centre and pour in the vegetable oil and eggs. Mix the eggs and oil with a whisk, gradually bringing in flour from the sides until it begins to thicken. Add the milk mixture little by little until all has been incorporated and the batter is smooth. Finally whisk in the water.

Pour the batter through a medium strainer into a bowl and refrigerate for at least 2 hours. (The resting time allows the batter to relax and the flour to absorb the liquids fully. Pancake batter may be made up to a day ahead and refrigerated.)

To cook, heat a 15–18cm (6–7in) frying pan. Add a very little oil. When the pan is hot, pour in just enough batter to cover the base of the pan.

Allow to cook on one side for 1–2 minutes, flip over on to the other side and continue to cook, until speckled and slightly golden.

Slide onto a plate and keep warm while you make the rest of the pancakes. You can stack one on top of the other as they can be peeled apart later but are best eaten fresh off the pan.

Per pancake: 72 kcals, 4g fat, 2g saturated fat, 8g carbohydrate, 0.21g sodium, 32mg calcium

Crème fraîche
If you can't buy crème fraîche or sour cream, this is a very simple recipe.

Juice of ½ lemon

8 tablespoons whipping cream

Salt and pepper

Water

Add the lemon juice to the cream and allow to thicken at room temperature for approximately 1 hour. Season with salt and pepper and then add water if necessary to achieve a good consistency.

Per recipe: 452 kcals, 47g fat, 30g saturated fat, 5g carbohydrate, 0.44g sodium, 80mg calcium

Cheddar cheese soufflé with chives

As flour is usually added to soufflés, coeliacs have had to resist the temptation of eating them. Now, using cornflour as the stabiliser, coeliacs can enjoy what they once could only admire! **Serves 6–8**

For the soufflé dish(es)

Knob of butter, melted

25g (1oz) fine dry gluten-free breadcrumbs (see page 118)

25g (1oz) butter

2 tablespoons cornflour

300ml (½ pint) milk

3 egg yolks and 4 egg whites, preferably free range

Salt

4 egg whites, preferably free range teaspoon gluten-free Dijon mustard

1 tablespoon finely chopped fresh chives

175g (6oz) mature Irish Cheddar cheese, grated

Large soufflé dish, 600ml (1 pint) capacity or 6–8 individual soufflé dishes, 7.5cm (2¾in) diameter x 4cm (1½in) deep

Prepare the soufflé dish or dishes by brushing the base and sides evenly with melted butter and dusting with a few fine gluten-free breadcrumbs. Preheat the oven to 200°C/400°F/gas mark 6 for individual soufflés or 180°C/350°F/gas mark 4 for a larger soufflé, and preheat a baking sheet.

Melt the butter in a heavy saucepan. When it stops foaming, add the cornflour and stir well. Cook gently for 2 minutes. Remove from the heat and whisk in the milk slowly, return to the heat and continue to whisk until the sauce boils and thickens. Remove from the heat again and beat in the egg yolks, one by one. Then add 1 teaspoon salt, the mustard, chives and all but 2 tablespoons of the cheese (reserved to

sprinkle over the top). The soufflé can be prepared ahead to this stage but the base mixture will need to be warmed again gently before the egg whites are folded in.

When you are ready to cook, pour the egg whites with a pinch of salt into a scrupulously clean copper, glass or stainless-steel bowl. Whisk, slowly at first and then faster until the whites are light and hold a stiff peak when you lift up the whisk. (The whites must not be whisked until you are about to cook the soufflé, otherwise they will lose volume.)

Stir about one-third of the whites into the cheese mixture to lighten it and then fold in the remainder very carefully using a spatula or tablespoon. Pour into the buttered and crumbed soufflé dish or dishes.

Sprinkle the reserved grated cheese on top and set the dish or dishes on the heated baking tray. Bake in the oven for 9–10 minutes for individual soufflés, or for 1 hour for a larger soufflé. Individual soufflés may be baked from frozen but will need a few minutes longer to cook. Don't be tempted to open the oven half way through the cooking as the soufflés may collapse. They should be well risen and golden on top yet slightly soft in the centre.

Serve immediately on hot plates (individual ones are served in their dishes).

Per serving: 251 kcals, 18g fat, 10g saturated fat, 9g carbohydrate, 0.68g sodium, 285mg calcium

Tomato, feta and pesto tart

An irresistible summer tart, which would go well with a salad of rocket leaves or a good green salad. You might like to substitute goat's cheese or buffalo mozzarella for feta occasionally. **Serves 6**

2 red peppers

1 tablespoon extra virgin olive oil

½ quantity Rosemary's savoury pastry (see page 150)

Rice flour, for dusting

Egg wash

175g (6oz) feta cheese

10 or more basil leaves

Salt and freshly ground pepper

Sugar (or balsamic vinegar)

8 tablespoons tomato fondue (see page 154)

2–3 tablespoons gluten-free pesto (see page 148)

1 x 18cm (7in) quiche tin or flan ring or 6 x 12cm (5in) low-sided tartlet tins

Preheat the oven to 250°C/475°F/gas mark 9.

First roast the red peppers. Place them on a baking tray and rub the surface with a little olive oil. Bake in the oven for 20–30 minutes, until they are soft and the skin blisters. Put them in a bowl and cover with clingfilm. Leave until cool enough to handle. Peel the peppers and remove the stalk and seeds but don't wash away the sweet juices. Cut into strips.

Reduce the oven temperature to 180°C/350°F/gas mark 4.

Make the savoury pastry following the recipe. Roll out the pastry on a very lightly rice-floured board. Line the tin with the pastry to a thickness of about 3mm (⅛in). Line to the top with parchment paper and fill with baking beans. Chill the pastry for a further 15–20 minutes and then bake the tart base blind for 15 minutes or until pale golden.

Remove the beans and paper, brush the tart shell with a little beaten egg and return to the oven for a further 2 minutes. This seals the pastry and helps to avoid a soggy bottom!

Crumble the feta cheese using the tips of your fingers and spread half the cheese over the base of the pastry. Arrange a layer of roasted red pepper strips and basil leaves on top. Season with a little salt and freshly ground black pepper and a sprinkle of sugar or balsamic vinegar (take care when seasoning as feta is quite salty). Cover with a layer of tomato fondue and spread the remaining feta cheese over.

Return the tart to the oven for 10–15 minutes until it is hot and bubbly. Drizzle the tart generously with pesto and serve immediately.

Per serving: 317 kcals, 23g fat, 11g saturated fat, 20g carbohydrate, 0.7g sodium, 141mg calcium

Pasta

4

Cannelloni

Coeliacs no longer have to miss out on these scrumptious rolls because this is a coeliac-friendly adaptation of a recipe in French Cookery School Book, *by Anne Willan and Jane Grigson.* **Serves 4 as a starter or 2 as a main course**

8 sheets of gluten-free dried lasagne

Salt and freshly ground black pepper

For the filling

450g (1lb) spinach, weighed without stalks

25g (1oz) butter

175g (6oz) chicken, minced

175g (6oz) lean pork, minced

2 small egg yolks, preferably free range

Good pinch of mace or freshly grated nutmeg

For the sauce

40g (1½oz) butter

40g (1½oz) cornflour

425ml (¾ pint) milk

Freshly grated nutmeg

300ml (10fl oz) single cream

15g (½oz) freshly grated Parmesan

For the topping

25g (1oz) freshly grated Parmesan

15g (¼oz) butter

Lasagne dish, 25 x 20cm (10 x 8in)

Bring 4.5 litres (8 pints) water to a rolling boil in a large pan and add 1–2 tablespoons salt. Add the lasagne sheets, two at a time, and stir to ensure they remain separate. Cover the pan just long enough to bring the water back to the boil and cook, uncovered, until the pasta is *al dente*. As soon as it is cooked, drain immediately and refresh in a bowl of cold water. Drain again and lay out flat on a clean tea-towel until required. Repeat with the remaining sheets.

Wash the spinach and shake off the excess water. Melt the butter in a large frying pan, toss in as much spinach as will fit easily and season with salt and freshly ground pepper. As soon as the spinach wilts and becomes tender, strain off the liquid, squeezing well if necessary between two plates until almost dry. Finely chop the spinach and allow it to cool.

Next make the sauce. Melt the butter in a heavy-based saucepan, stir in the cornflour and cook for 2 minutes. Pour in the milk, bring to the boil, whisking all the time, season with salt, freshly ground pepper and grated nutmeg and cook for 2 minutes. Add enough cream to make a fairly thick sauce and remove from the heat.

Mix the minced chicken and pork together with the cooled chopped spinach. Add the egg yolks and 300ml (½ pint) of the sauce. Season well with salt, freshly ground pepper and ground mace or grated nutmeg.

Preheat the oven to 180°C/350°F/gas mark 4.

To assemble, butter the lasagne dish lightly. Fill each lasagne square with 1–2 tablespoons of the filling. Moisten the edges with water and roll them up, starting from one of the narrower sides, to form a thick tube. Place the cannelloni side by side in the dish, in such a manner that the join is underneath.

Reheat the sauce and stir in the remaining cream and the parmesan. Taste and adjust the seasoning if necessary. Spoon the sauce over the cannelloni – it should cover them completely.

Sprinkle parmesan over the top and dot with butter. (The cannelloni can be prepared ahead and reheated, provided each component is cold when it is put together, so keep them in the fridge. They can be frozen and will keep for 2 months.)

Cover with foil and bake in the oven for 40–45 minutes. Ten minutes before the end of cooking remove the foil lid so that the cheese browns and is bubbly on top.

Per serving (starter): 566 kcals, 29g fat, 16g saturated fat, 44g carbohydrate, 0.75g sodium, 502mg calcium

Macaroni cheese with smoked salmon

Delicious on its own, but also the perfect foil for some tasty additions. Macaroni cheese needs a new image, so forget the old Pyrex and use a really stylish ovenproof dish! **Serves 6**

Salt and freshly ground black pepper

225g (8oz) gluten-free macaroni

50g (2oz) butter

50g (2oz) cornflour

850ml (1½ pints) boiling milk

¼ teaspoon gluten-free Dijon mustard

1 tablespoon chopped fresh parsley (optional)

150g (5oz) mature Cheddar cheese, grated

110g (4oz) good-quality smoked salmon, preferably organic, chopped

1.2 litre (2 pint) pie dish

Bring 4.5 litres (8 pints) water to a rolling boil in a large pan and add 1–2 tablespoons salt. Tip the pasta in all at once and stir well to ensure the pieces remain separate. Cover the pan just long enough to bring the water back to the boil and cook, uncovered, until *al dente*. As soon as the pasta is cooked, drain it immediately.

Meanwhile melt the butter in a heavy-bottomed saucepan, add the cornflour and cook, stirring occasionally, for 1–2 minutes. Remove from the heat. Whisk in the milk gradually, then bring to the boil, stirring all the time. Add the mustard, parsley (if using) and cheese and season with salt and freshly ground pepper to taste. Add the cooked gluten-free macaroni, bring back to the boil and stir in the chopped smoked salmon. Serve immediately.

Although macaroni cheese is perfect just as the pasta has been mixed with the creamy sauce, it reheats very successfully, provided the pasta is not overcooked in the first place. It is very good served with cold meat, particularly ham, or layered with little chunks of gluten-free salami, or gluten-free chorizo, smoked mackerel or chargrilled vegetables.

Per serving: 431 kcals, 20g fat, 12g saturated fat, 46g carbohydrate, 0.82g sodium, 378mg calcium

Spaghetti with tomato, chilli, mozzarella and basil

The sauce for this tasty pasta dish can be prepared in advance and reheated later. If you prefer, use Parmesan cheese rather than mozzarella. **Serves 4**

350g (12oz) gluten-free spaghetti

Extra virgin olive oil

Salt and freshly ground black pepper

175g (6oz) buffalo mozzarella, thinly sliced

Fresh basil leaves

For the sauce

4 tablespoons extra virgin olive oil

2 large garlic cloves, cut into slivers

2 whole dried chillies, crushed

900g (2lb) very ripe tomatoes, peeled and chopped

Pinch of sugar, if necessary

Fresh basil leaves, torn

First make the sauce. Heat the olive oil in a wide saucepan, add the sliced garlic and cook for a few seconds, then add the chillies and the chopped tomatoes. Cook on a high heat at first and then reduce to a medium heat and cook for 15–20 minutes. Season with salt, freshly ground pepper and a pinch of sugar. Add lots of freshly torn basil leaves to the tomato sauce towards the end of cooking.

Bring 4.5 litres (8 pints) water to a rolling boil in a large saucepan and add 1–2 tablespoons salt. Tip the pasta in all at once and stir well to ensure the pieces remain separate. Cover the pan just long enough to bring the water back to the boil and cook, uncovered, until *al dente*. As soon as the pasta is cooked, drain it immediately, toss in a little olive oil and season with salt and freshly ground pepper. Add the pasta to the bubbling sauce and continue to cook for a further minute. Taste and adjust the seasoning if necessary.

Transfer to a hot serving dish, with the slices of buffalo mozzarella melting on top and a few extra basil leaves. Serve at once.

Per serving: 571 kcals, 25g fat, 8g saturated fat, 72g carbohydrate, 0.46g sodium, 306mg calcium

Gnocchi with pesto

Not, of course, pasta but another fabulous Italian dish that coeliacs have usually had to forgo. This gluten-free version of these potato dumplings is delightfully light. **Serves 6 as a light lunch**

1kg (2¼lb) unpeeled potatoes, preferably Golden Wonder or Kerr's Pink	50g (2oz) butter
	275g (10oz) potato flour
Salt and freshly ground black pepper	Gluten-free pesto (see page 148)
2 egg yolks, preferably free range, lightly beaten	75g (3oz) Parmesan, freshly grated

Scrub the potatoes well and place in a saucepan of cold water with a good pinch of salt. Cover and bring to the boil. When the potatoes are about half cooked, say 15 minutes approximately for 'old' potatoes, strain off two-thirds of the water, replace the lid on the pan, put on a low heat and allow the potatoes to steam until cooked. Peel immediately by just pulling off the skins, so you have as little waste as possible. This way the potatoes will be as 'dry' as possible and most suitable for making gnocchi.

Push the peeled potatoes through a mouli-légume or a potato ricer into a large bowl to produce light, fluffy and lump-free potatoes. Add the egg yolks, butter, a generous pinch of salt and freshly ground black pepper. Mix well to combine and then, slowly at first, stir in about half of the potato flour. Using the 'heel' of your hand, knead lightly, ensuring all the flour is evenly distributed. Continue to add more of the potato flour in this manner to produce a firm dough.

Bring a large pan of water to the boil and add a good pinch of salt. Take a small piece of the dough and form into a little ball to represent a gnocchi. Reduce the heat so that the water is simmering and cook the piece for a couple of minutes. The gnocchi is almost ready when it floats to the surface of the water. Allow it to 'bob up and down' on the surface for a further minute, then remove. The dough, if it is too dry, will produce a heavy, stodgy end-product; if it is too wet, it will fall apart in the water while it is cooking. The correct balance between potato flour and egg is vital, so adjust accordingly. Taste the gnocchi and adjust the seasoning if necessary.

When you are happy with the flavour and texture of the gnocchi, divide the potato dough into four equal sections. Lightly potato-flour the work surface and roll out each section of dough to form a 'log' 1.5cm (¾in) thick. Cut each 'log' into equal sections, each measuring 2.5cm (1in) long. Refrigerate the pieces for 15–20 minutes to make the dough easier to handle. After this time, form the traditional shape of the gnocchi by gently pressing each 'log' against the back of the prongs of a fork. The little shape is then curved slightly with your fingers, resulting in a dumpling that is hollow, with a number of shallow indentations. These indentations are perfect for catching some of the chosen sauce.

Bring the water in the pan back to the boil and drop in about 15 gnocchi. Reduce the temperature, so that the water is simmering, and allow them to cook as described above. Remove from the pan with a slotted spoon and leave to drain thoroughly in a colander if necessary. Cover the gnocchi and keep warm while you cook the remainder.

Pile the gnocchi into a warm serving dish or six individual dishes, drizzle liberally with pesto and sprinkle with freshly grated Parmesan. Serve immediately with gluten-free bread and a green salad for a delicious summery lunch.

Per serving: 709 kcals, 42g fat, 13g saturated fat, 67g carbohydrate, 0.45g sodium, 333mg calcium

Rosemary gnocchi with tomato sauce

Mix 2–3 teaspoons freshly chopped rosemary with the potato flour and add to the potatoes. Prepare the gnocchi as before. Serve with tomato fondue (see page 154) that has been put through a mouli-légume to produce a smooth sauce. Sprinkle with freshly grated Parmesan and serve immediately.

Per serving: 519 kcals, 18g fat, 8g saturated fat, 77g carbohydrate, 0.69g sodium, 208mg calcium

Spicy aubergine lasagne

This is great for parties as it can be prepared in advance and reheats successfully. Don't be put off by the number of components to the dish — it is really tasty. Just take care not to overcook it. **Serves 8–10**

1 quantity gluten-free
    Béchamel sauce (page 150)
A little milk
1 quantity spicy aubergines
1 quantity creamed spinach
1 quantity leeks and yellow
    peppers

375g (13oz) dried plain gluten-
    free lasagne
Salt and freshly ground pepper
50g (2oz) grated Parmesan
Few knobs of butter
Lasagne dish, 28 x 20cm
    (11 x 8in)

First make the gluten-free béchamel sauce, adding a little extra milk to ensure it is not too thick for good coverage. Follow the recipes for spicy aubergine, creamed spinach and leek and yellow pepper layers. Set aside until required.

Preheat the oven to 180°C/350°F/gas mark 4.

Bring 4.5 litres (8 pints) water to a rolling boil in a large pan and add 1–2 tablespoons salt. Cook 3 or 4 sheets of pasta at a time, stir to keep them separate and cook for just 30 seconds after the water comes back to the boil. Remove, put into a bowl of cold water, then drain on a clean tea-towel.

Taste each component to ensure it is delicious and well seasoned. Spread a little béchamel sauce on the base of the dish, cover with a layer of barely overlapping pasta sheets and half the spicy aubergine mix. Spread the creamed spinach over the spicy aubergine and add another layer of pasta. Spread with the other half of the spiced aubergine and then more pasta. Add the leeks and yellow peppers next, then more pasta, ending with a layer of béchamel sauce and a good sprinkling of Parmesan cheese. Ensure all the pasta is under the sauce.

Dot with a few little knobs of butter and wipe the edges of the dish clean. (The dish may be prepared ahead to this point and refrigerated for a few days or frozen for up to 3 months.)

Bake in the oven for 35 minutes or until the lasagne is golden and bubbly on top. Allow the lasagne to rest for about 10 minutes so that the layers compact slightly. Serve from the dish.

Per serving: 689 kcals, 43g fat, 15g saturated fat, 63g carbohydrate, 0.76g sodium, 422mg calcium

Spicy aubergine layer

800g (1¾lb) aubergines
225ml (8fl oz) vegetable oil
2.5cm (1in) cube fresh ginger, coarsely chopped
6 large garlic cloves, coarsely crushed
50 ml (2fl oz) water
1 teaspoon whole fennel seeds
½ teaspoon whole cumin seeds

350g (12oz) very ripe tomatoes, peeled and finely chopped, or 400g (14oz) tinned tomatoes
1 teaspoon sugar, less if using fresh tomatoes
1 tablespoon coriander seeds, freshly ground
¼ teaspoon ground turmeric
⅓ teaspoon cayenne pepper
1 teaspoon salt
50g (2oz) raisins

Cut the aubergines into 2cm (¾in) thick slices. Heat 175 ml (6fl oz) of the oil in a deep 25.5–30 cm (10–12in) frying pan. When hot and almost smoking, add a few aubergine slices and cook until golden and tender on both sides. Remove and drain on a wire rack over a baking sheet. Repeat with the remaining aubergines, adding more oil if necessary.

Put the ginger, garlic and water into a blender or food-processor. Blend until fairly smooth.

Heat the remaining oil in the frying pan. When hot, add the fennel and cumin seeds (be careful not to let them burn). Stir for just a few seconds, then add the chopped tomatoes, the ginger and garlic mixture, sugar, coriander, turmeric, cayenne and salt. Simmer, stirring occasionally, until the spice mixture thickens slightly, about 5–6 minutes.

Return the fried aubergine slices to the pan and add the raisins. Mix gently with the spicy sauce. Cover the pan, reduce the heat to very low and cook for a further 5–8 minutes.

Creamed spinach layer

700g (1½lb) fresh spinach, weighed without stalks
25–40g (1–1½oz) butter
175–250ml (6–8 fl oz) single cream

Gluten-free roux (see page 150) (optional)
Salt and freshly ground black pepper
A little freshly grated nutmeg

Wash the spinach and shake off the excess water. Put into a heavy pan over a low heat, season and cover tightly. After a few minutes, stir and replace the lid. After about 5–8 minutes, strain off the copious amount of liquid that spinach releases and press between 2 plates until almost dry. Return to the pan, increase the heat and add the butter and cream. Bring to the boil, stir well and thicken with a little gluten-free roux if desired, or stir over the heat until the spinach has absorbed most of the cream. Season with salt, pepper and freshly grated nutmeg to taste.

Leek and yellow pepper layer

4 leeks
2 yellow peppers
10g (½oz) butter
1 tablespoon extra virgin olive oil

1 tablespoon water
Salt and freshly ground black pepper

Wash the leeks and slice into 5mm (¼in) rounds. Quarter and core the peppers and cut into 5mm (¼in) thick slices at an angle. Heat the butter and oil in a heavy-based pan, toss in the leeks and add a little water. Season with salt and freshly ground black pepper. Cover and sweat on a gentle heat for about 8 minutes or until tender. Add the peppers, toss and add a drop more water if necessary, then continue to cook until the peppers are soft. Taste and adjust the seasoning if necessary.

Buckwheat lasagne squares with mushroom and buffalo mozzarella

Buckwheat is entirely coeliac-friendly: don't be put off by its colour and enjoy the taste! **Serves 4 as a light lunch**

150g (5oz) buckwheat flour
25g (1oz) soya flour
25g (1oz) tapioca flour
1 teaspoon xanthan gum
Salt
2 eggs, preferably free range
2–3 tablespoons milk
1 quantity Mushroom à la Crème (see page 151)

1 x 140g (4½oz) ball buffalo mozzarella
50g (2oz) freshly grated Parmesan
Freshly chopped flat parsley

Ovenproof dish, 20 x 25cm (8 x 10in)

Sift the buckwheat flour, soya flour, tapioca flour, xanthan gum and salt into a bowl. In another bowl whisk the eggs and add the milk. Make a well in the centre of the flours and pour in the egg and milk mixture. Combine the two using a fork, adding a little more milk very gradually, being careful not to add too much liquid. Knead the dough using the heel of your hand for at least 5 minutes to achieve a smooth texture. Cover the dough with a bowl and leave to stand for 10 minutes before rolling out.

Meanwhile make the Mushroom à la Crème.

Divide the dough in half and roll out very thinly. Cut into 10cm (4in) squares and place on sheets of parchment paper until required.

Preheat the oven to 180°C/350°F/gas mark 4.

Bring 2.5 litres (4 pints) water to a rolling boil and add 1 tablespoon salt. Cook the pasta squares 2 or 3 at a time, uncovered, for 5 minutes or until *al dente*. Scoop out using a 'spider' or slotted spoon. Refresh in cold water, drain and lay on a clean tea-towel.

Place one layer of buckwheat pasta squares in the ovenproof dish. Top with 3 tablespoons Mushroom à la Crème and 3 or 4 slices of the mozzarella. Put another layer of pasta on top, more mozzarella and then a final layer of pasta. Spoon a little more mushroom over the top, sprinkle with freshly grated Parmesan and reheat in the oven for about 10 minutes until hot and bubbly.

Sprinkle with freshly chopped parsley and serve with a good green salad.

Per serving: 813 kcals, 51g fat, 31g saturated fat, 66g carbohydrate, 1.04g sodium, 459mg calcium

Baked pasta with bacon and spring onion

A simple supper dish, which you could make even more delicious and nutritious with the addition of some sautéed mushrooms. Serve warm with a green salad. **Serves 6**

Salt and freshly ground black pepper

225g (8oz) gluten-free pasta shapes, e.g. penne

6–8 bacon rashers

2 teaspoons extra virgin olive oil

150g (5oz) onions, chopped

110g (4oz) spring onions, green tops included, chopped

4 eggs, preferably free range

300ml (½ pint) milk

350ml (12fl oz) single cream

2 teaspoons freshly chopped marjoram

50g (2oz) freshly grated Parmesan, plus extra for sprinkling

Ovenproof gratin dish, 20 x 25cm (8 x 10in)

Preheat the oven to 180°C/350°F/gas mark 4.

Bring 4.5 litres (8 pints) water to a rolling boil in a large and add 1–2 tablespoons of salt. Tip the pasta in all at once and stir well to ensure the shapes remain separate. Cover the pan just long enough to bring the water back to the boil and cook, uncovered, until the pasta is *al dente*. Immediately drain it in a colander and run cold water through it to cool. Drain again thoroughly.

Cut the bacon into 2.5cm (1in) lardons. Heat the olive oil in a large non-stick frying pan. Add the bacon and cook until almost crisp. Drain the bacon on kitchen paper. Sweat the onions and spring onions gently in the oil and bacon fat for about 10 minutes, remove and leave to cool.

Whisk the eggs in a large bowl, then add the milk, cream, marjoram, Parmesan, cooled onions and spring onions. Season with salt and freshly ground black pepper. Put the pasta in the base of the ovenproof gratin dish. Sprinkle a layer of bacon lardons over the top and cover with the egg mixture.

Sprinkle extra cheese over the top and bake in the oven for 30–35 minutes or until the surface is golden and firm.

Per serving: 464 kcals, 26g fat, 13g saturated fat, 39g carbohydrate, 0.65g sodium, 319mg calcium

Penne with spicy broccoli and toasted crumbs

A fabulous way of including more vegetarian options in your diet! Broccoli is particularly good with the salty tang of anchovies. **Serves 4**

450g (1lb) gluten-free penne

450g (1lb) broccoli florets

4 tablespoons olive oil

1 large garlic clove, crushed

½ teaspoon dried red chilli flakes

4 tinned anchovies, coarsely chopped (optional)

4 tablespoons freshly grated Parmesan

For the toasted crumbs

6 tablespoons extra virgin olive oil

75g (3oz) gluten-free white breadcrumbs (see page 118)

Make the toasted crumbs. Heat the oil in a large, heavy-based frying pan, add the breadcrumbs and stir constantly over a high heat for 5–6 minutes or until the crumbs become crisp and golden. Drain on kitchen paper and set aside.

Bring 4.5 litres (8 pints) water to the boil and add 1–2 tablespoons of salt. Tip the penne in all at once, stirring well to ensure all the shapes remain separate. Cover the pan just long enough to bring the water back to the boil and cook, uncovered, until the pasta is *al dente*. Immediately drain it but reserve a little of the cooking water in case you need to adjust the consistency of the sauce.

Peel the stems of the broccoli and chop finely. Set aside. Divide the florets into small pieces. Bring 600ml (1 pint) water to the boil, add 1½ teaspoons salt and the florets. Cook, uncovered, for 5–6 minutes. Drain while the broccoli still has bite.

Heat the oil in a large frying pan over a medium heat. Add the garlic, chilli, broccoli stalks and anchovies (if using). Cook for 5 minutes or until soft. Add the broccoli florets to the pan, toss to combine and heat through. Mix the broccoli mixture through the pasta with a little of the reserved cooking water. Transfer to a warm serving dish and scatter with the toasted golden bread-crumbs. Taste for seasoning, sprinkle generously with the Parmesan and serve immediately.

Per serving: 731 kcals, 35g fat, 6g saturated fat, 92g carbohydrate, 0.26g sodium, 202mg calcium

5

Main Courses

Piperonata

This vegetable stew is so much more than a main course: use it as a topping for pizzas, as a sauce for pasta, grilled fish or meat and as a filling for omelettes and pancakes. It keeps in the fridge for 3–4 days and freezes perfectly. **Serves 6**

2 tablespoons extra virgin olive oil
1 garlic clove, crushed
1 onion, sliced
2 red peppers
2 green or yellow peppers

6 large tomatoes (dark red and very ripe)
Salt and freshly ground black pepper
Sugar
Fresh basil leaves

Heat the olive oil in a large, heavy-based flameproof casserole. Add the garlic and cook for a few seconds, then add the sliced onion, toss in the oil and allow to soften over a low heat, covered with the lid, while you prepare the peppers.

Halve the peppers and remove the seeds. Carefully cut into quarters and then into strips across rather than lengthwise. Add to the casserole and stir around in the oil; replace the lid and continue to cook.

Meanwhile peel the tomatoes (first scald in boiling water for 10 seconds, pour off the water and peel immediately). Slice the tomatoes and add to the casserole, season with salt, freshly ground black pepper, sugar and a few leaves of fresh basil if available. Cook until the vegetables are just soft, say about 30 minutes.

Per serving: 87 kcals, 4g fat, 0g saturated fat, 11g carbohydrate, 0.15g sodium, 23mg calcium

Piperade

For a delicious supper dish, put a bed of piperonata into a shallow ovenproof dish. Crack an egg into the centre and cook in a preheated oven, 180°C/350°F/gas mark 4, for about 10 minutes. Scatter with flat parsley and serve.

Oven-roasted vegetable and pesto pizza

Roasting vegetables concentrates their flavour and makes them crisp and sweet, as well as irresistible and healthy!

Makes 2 x 20cm (8in) pizzas

1 aubergine
Salt and freshly ground black pepper
1 courgette
1 red onion
1 red pepper
1 yellow pepper

3 tablespoons extra virgin olive oil
1 quantity tomato fondue (see page 154)
½ quantity gluten-free pizza base (see page 149)
1–2 tablespoons gluten-free pesto (see page 148)

Preheat the oven to 200°C/400°F/gas mark 6.

Prepare the vegetables for the topping of the pizza: cut the aubergine into 1cm (½in) chunks, sprinkle with salt and leave to drain for 15 minutes. Rinse to remove the excess salt and pat dry with kitchen paper. Cut the courgette and red onion into 1cm (½in) chunks. Halve the red and yellow peppers, remove the seeds carefully, cut into quarters and then into 1cm (½in) chunks. Put the vegetables into a bowl, drizzle with oil and freshly ground black pepper. Toss to coat.

Arrange the vegetables as a single layer on a baking sheet and roast in the oven for about 40 minutes until golden and crispy. Sprinkle on a little salt towards the end of cooking.

Make the tomato fondue and cook it over a low heat until reduced and concentrated. Adjust the seasoning if necessary.

Follow the recipe for gluten-free pizza base. Roll out as two rounds and bake for 8 minutes. Remove from the oven and spread the bases with the concentrated tomato fondue, then the roasted vegetables, and return to the oven for a further 10–15 minutes until hot, bubbly and cooked through. Drizzle with a little pesto. Serve immediately with a good green salad.

Per pizza: 812 kcals, 37g fat, 6g saturated fat, 108g carbohydrate, 1.13g sodium, 241mg calcium

Ricotta, spinach and parmesan tart

A delicious, rich tart – wonderful served at lunch, on summer picnics or as a pretty impressive first course for a dinner party! Use a yellow rather than a red pepper if you prefer. **Serves 6**

1 red pepper

Extra virgin olive oil

1 quantity Rosemary's savoury
    pastry (see page 150)

Egg wash

For the filling

225g (8oz) baby spinach
    leaves, destalked

25g (1oz) butter

Salt and freshly ground black
    pepper

25g (1oz) pine nuts

2 eggs, preferably free range,
    lightly beaten

50ml (2fl oz) single cream

275g (10oz) ricotta

50g (2oz) Parmesan, grated

Freshly grated nutmeg

Quiche tin or flan ring with
    removable base, 18cm (7in)
    diameter and 4cm (1½in)
    deep

Preheat the oven to 250°C/475°F/gas mark 9.

Rub the red pepper with a little olive oil, place it on a baking tray and roast in the oven for 20–30 minutes, until it is soft and the skin blisters. Put in a bowl, cover with clingfilm and leave until cool enough to handle. Peel the pepper and remove the stalk and seeds but don't wash away the lovely juices.

Reduce the oven temperature to 180°C/350°F/gas mark 4.

Make the gluten-free savoury pastry following the recipe. Line the tin with the pastry, fill with baking beans and bake blind for 20 minutes in the oven. Remove the beans, egg-wash the base and return to the oven for a further 2 minutes. This seals the pastry and helps to avoid a soggy bottom!

Wash the destalked spinach in a colander. Melt the butter in a large frying pan, toss in the spinach and season with salt and freshly ground black pepper. As soon as the spinach wilts and becomes tender, strain off the excess liquid. Squeeze the spinach very well between two plates and chop it.

Put the pine nuts on a baking sheet and roast in the oven for about 8 minutes. Be careful: they burn very easily.

Whisk together the eggs and cream. Add the ricotta and mix well. Gently stir in the chopped spinach, toasted pine nuts and the grated Parmesan. Slice the roasted red pepper (reserving a few slices for the top of the tart) and stir through the filling. Season with salt, freshly ground black pepper and a little freshly grated nutmeg.

Pour the filling into the cooked pastry case. Arrange the reserved slices of red pepper on top and bake for 30 minutes until firm and golden.

Serve warm with a good green salad.

Per serving: 573 kcals, 42g fat, 23g saturated fat, 34g carbohydrate, 0.71g sodium, 336mg calcium

Thyme polenta, goat's cheese and roasted vegetables

Polenta, made from cornmeal, is a good foil for rich meat or game stews or a base for tasty toppings (roast peppers, caramelised onions, pesto or tapenade). **Serves 6–8**

1.8 litres (3 pints) water
2 level teaspoons salt
225g (8oz) coarse polenta flour (cornmeal)
3 tablespoons freshly chopped thyme
15g (½oz) butter

For the filling
3 red onions, cut into chunks
8 large mushrooms, quartered

4 tablespoons extra virgin olive oil
1 tablespoon balsamic vinegar
25g (1oz) pine nuts
175g (6oz) soft goat's cheese, crumbled

Swiss roll tin or lasagne dish, 23 x 18 x 5cm (9 x 7 x 2in)

Put the water into a deep, heavy-based saucepan and bring to the boil, add the salt, then sprinkle in the polenta flour very slowly, letting it slip gradually through your fingers, whisking all the time (this should take 3–4 minutes). Bring to the boil and when it starts to 'erupt like a volcano' reduce the heat to the absolute minimum – use a heat diffuser mat if you have one.

Cook for about 40 minutes, stirring regularly. If you stir constantly on a slightly higher heat, the cooking time can be reduced to about 20 minutes, but polenta is more digestible if cooked more slowly over a longer period. (Try using a whisk at the beginning, but as soon as the polenta comes to the boil, change to a flat-bottomed wooden spoon.) The polenta is cooked when it is very thick but not solid and comes away from the sides of the pot as you stir.

As soon as the polenta is cooked, stir in the chopped thyme and butter. Pour the polenta into the Swiss roll tin or lasagne dish and leave to set for several hours or overnight. Store in the fridge. When the polenta has set (it needs to be firm enough to be cut), preheat the oven to 200°C/400°F/ gas mark 6.

Toss the red onions and mushrooms in the olive oil and balsamic vinegar, then tip onto a roasting tray. Roast for about 25 minutes until golden. Watch the edges carefully as they burn easily.

Roast the pine nuts in the oven for 5 minutes. Watch carefully to ensure they don't burn.

To serve, turn the set polenta onto a clean chopping board and cut into slices, disks or diamonds 1–2cm (½–¾in) thick and char-grill or pan-grill. (Put the polenta directly onto the bars of the grill on the highest heat without oil and cook until hot through and grill-marked on each side.) Alternatively, sauté in a little olive oil or butter. Stack the polenta up with alternate layers of roasted vegetables and goat's cheese between them. It is absolutely delicious served with some rocket leaves and toasted pine nuts.

Per serving: 353 kcals, 18g fat, 5g saturated fat, 39g carbohydrate, 0.82g sodium, 94mg calcium

Baked courgette and rosemary risotto

Rice is gluten-free and really versatile. It is the external layers that contain vitamins B1, B2 and minerals, so brown rice is nutritionally superior to white rice. **Serves 8–10**

350g (12oz) Arborio, Carnaroli or Vilano Nano rice
Salt and freshly ground black pepper
5 tablespoons extra virgin olive oil
275g (10oz) onions, finely chopped
2 garlic cloves, finely chopped
350g (12oz) courgettes, grated on the coarsest part of the grater

3 medium eggs, preferably free range, beaten
4 tablespoons single cream
2–3 tablespoons freshly chopped rosemary
¼ teaspoon freshly grated nutmeg
175g (6oz) Gruyère cheese, grated
1 quantity tomato fondue (see page 154)

20cm (8in) spring-form tin

Prepare the spring-form tin, brushing it evenly with olive oil.

Preheat the oven to 180°C/350°F/gas mark 4.

Cook the risotto rice in a large pan of boiling salted water for 8 minutes and then drain thoroughly. Set aside.

Heat the oil in a heavy-based saucepan and sweat the onions and garlic until soft but not coloured. Add the courgettes, season with salt and freshly ground black pepper and cook on a high heat for 5 minutes. Transfer the onion, garlic and courgette mixture to a mixing bowl and leave to cool.

Add the beaten eggs, par-cooked rice, cream, rosemary, nutmeg, salt and freshly ground black pepper and mix well.

Pour this mixture into the prepared tin, sprinkle with the grated Gruyère cheese and bake in the oven for about 40 minutes or until the surface is golden brown.

Allow to cool in the tin for 5 minutes before turning out.

Try this baked risotto warm with tomato fondue. It is also delicious served with a mixed leaf salad and a little tomato salad – great for picnics or packed lunches.

Per serving: 430 kcals, 22g fat, 8g saturated fat, 47g carbohydrate, 0.36g sodium, 271mg calcium

Stuffed mushrooms with pancetta and pine nuts

Serve these yummy mushrooms for lunch with a little crusty gluten-free bread or to accompany pan-grilled chicken breast or a juicy steak with crispy potatoes. **Serves 4**

10g (½oz) butter, softened
4 large flat mushrooms, stalks carefully removed and reserved for the filling
For the filling
1 tablespoon olive oil
110g (4oz) gluten-free pancetta, rind removed, cut into 1cm (½in) lardons
1 onion, finely chopped
4 mushroom stalks, chopped
1 garlic clove, crushed

Salt and freshly ground black pepper
25g (1oz) gluten-free breadcrumbs (see page 118)
1 egg yolk, preferably free range
25g (1oz) pine nuts, chopped
½ teaspoon freshly grated lemon rind
1 tablespoon freshly chopped thyme leaves

Lightly butter an ovenproof serving dish, and arrange the mushrooms in a single layer in it.

Preheat the oven to 180°C/350°F/gas mark 4.

Heat the oil in a heavy-based frying pan and crisp off the chopped pancetta. Remove, reduce the heat and sweat the onions gently in the oil and pancetta fat for about 10 minutes. Add the chopped mushroom stalks and garlic. Season with a little salt and pepper and continue to cook until the mushrooms wilt and all the moisture has evaporated. Allow them to cool slightly, stir in the gluten-free breadcrumbs and return the pancetta to the pan. Whisk the egg yolk in a bowl and add the chopped pine nuts, lemon rind and chopped thyme. Mix all the ingredients for the filling together, taste and adjust the seasoning if necessary. Season the flat mushrooms with a little salt and freshly ground pepper and divide the stuffing evenly between them. The dish may be prepared ahead to this point.

Bake the mushrooms in the oven for about 15–20 minutes or until they are cooked through, but still nice and juicy.

Per serving: 255 kcals, 21g fat, 7g saturated fat, 6g carbohydrate, 0.6g sodium, 39mg calcium

Bubbly cheddar cheese and cauliflower gratin

A wonderful tasty dish, one that can be prepared in advance. Select a cauliflower with as many leaves attached as possible, as they too have some flavour. **Serves 8**

1 medium cauliflower with green leaves
Salt and freshly ground black pepper
For the mornay sauce
600ml (1 pint) milk with a dash of single cream
1 onion, sliced
3–4 slices of carrot
6 peppercorns
Fresh thyme or parsley
Gluten-free roux (see page 150)
150g (5oz) Cheddar cheese, grated, or a mixture of Gruyère, Parmesan and Cheddar
½ teaspoon gluten-free Dijon mustard
Chopped flat parsley, to garnish

Preheat the oven to 230°C/450°F/gas mark 8.

Remove the outer leaves and wash the cauliflower and the leaves well. Put no more than 2.5cm (1in) water in a saucepan just large enough to take the cauliflower; add a little salt and bring to the boil. Chop the leaves into small pieces and cut the cauliflower into quarters. Place the cauliflower on top of the green leaves in the pan, cover and simmer until the cauliflower is cooked, which takes about 15 minutes. Test by piercing the stalk with a knife: there should be just a little resistance. Transfer the cauliflower and the leaves to an ovenproof dish.

Meanwhile, make the mornay sauce. Put the cold milk into a small saucepan with the onion, carrot, peppercorns and herb. Bring to the boil, simmer for 3–4 minutes, remove from the heat and leave to infuse for 10 minutes.

Strain out the vegetables and herbs, bring the milk back to the boil and thicken with a little gluten-free roux to give a light coating consistency. Add most of the grated cheese, reserving enough to sprinkle over the dish, and the Dijon mustard. Season with salt and pepper. Spoon the sauce over the cauliflower and sprinkle with the remaining cheese. The dish may be prepared ahead to this point.

Put into the oven, or under a preheated grill, to brown. If you have prepared the dish in advance and allowed it to get completely cold, it will take 20–25 minutes to reheat in the oven. Flash under a hot grill if not sufficiently browned. **Serve** sprinkled with chopped parsley.

Per serving: 299 kcals, 22g fat, 14g saturated fat, 17g carbohydrate, 0.43g sodium, 249mg calcium

Cauliflower cheese soup

Follow the recipe above, but instead of browning in the oven or under the grill, liquidise the lot with any leftover cauliflower cooking water and enough light chicken stock (about 850ml/1½ pints) to give a nice consistency. Taste and adjust the seasoning if necessary. Serve with gluten-free croûtons (made from 1cm (½in) thick slices of gluten-free white bread, toasted and cut into chunks), diced Cheddar cheese and chopped flat parsley.

Stuffed red peppers with pesto rice and cherry tomatoes

These make an impressive and tasty starter, a vegetarian main course or an accompaniment for meat-eaters! **Serves 2 as a main course or 4 as a starter**

4 even-sized red peppers,
    Spanish if available

Olive oil

For the filling

1½ tablespoons olive oil

2 onions, chopped

Salt and freshly ground black
    pepper

2 garlic cloves, chopped

250g (9oz) cooked Basmati rice

2–3 tablespoons gluten-free
    pesto (see page 148)

16 cherry tomatoes

40g (1½oz) pine nuts

2 tablespoons fresh, chopped
    flat parsley

**For the buttered parsley
gluten-free crumbs**

50g (2oz) butter

110g (4oz) gluten-free
    breadcrumbs (see page 118)

25g (1oz) fresh, chopped flat
    parsley

Preheat the oven to 160°C/325°F/gas mark 3.

Halve the peppers by inserting the knife under the stalk. Cut around the sides and the base of each pepper. Open out from the bottom. The core may then be removed intact, so there is virtually no waste and the natural container of the pepper is preserved. Shake out any remaining seeds and remove the protruding membrane or flesh.

Brush an ovenproof dish with olive oil and rub a little more around the peppers. Place the peppers cut-side up in the dish.

To make the filling, heat the olive oil in a heavy-based frying pan and fry the onions for 1–2 minutes until they start to become golden brown at the edges. Season with salt and pepper. Add the garlic and continue to cook for a further minute. Remove from the pan and leave to cool.

Meanwhile, make the buttered parsley gluten-free crumbs. Melt the butter in a pan and stir in the gluten-free breadcrumbs and chopped parsley. Remove from the heat immediately and allow to cool.

Mix the cooked Basmati rice with the pesto in a bowl. Quarter the cherry tomatoes, chop the pine nuts and add to the bowl with the cooled onions and garlic. Stir in the chopped parsley, taste and adjust the seasoning if necessary.

Divide the mixture between the halved peppers and top with the buttered parsley gluten-free crumbs. The recipe can be prepared ahead up to this point, but make sure all your ingredients are cold before mixing together and stuffing the peppers.

Cover the dish with aluminium foil and bake in the oven for 50–60 minutes, removing the foil 15 minutes before the end of cooking to brown the gluten-free crumbs on top. The peppers should still be *al dente*, otherwise the sides may collapse.

Per serving: 475 kcals, 29g fat, 9g saturated fat, 49g carbohydrate, 0.35g sodium, 97mg calcium

Indian spiced vegetable pakoras with raita

Pakoras are crispy vegetables cooked in a spicy gluten-free batter which are good served piping hot with the cooling yogurt raita. **Serves 6**

For the spiced vegetables

1 thin aubergine cut into 5mm (¼in) slices

Salt

2 medium courgettes, cut into 2.5cm (1in) slices (or, if they are very large, cut the slices into quarters or batons)

4–6 asparagus spears, when in season

12 cauliflower or broccoli florets

6 large or 12 small flat mushrooms, cut in half

4–6 spring onions, sliced into 7–10cm (3–4in) lengths if they are large

For the batter

175g (6oz) chickpea or gram flour

1 tablespoon fresh chopped coriander

2 teaspoons curry powder (ensure it is gluten-free)

1 tablespoon olive oil

1 tablespoon freshly squeezed lemon juice,

175–250ml (6–8fl oz) iced water

vegetable oil for deep frying

To garnish

Lemon wedges

Coriander or parsley

Raita (see recipe), to serve

First make the raita, because it should be served chilled.

Put the aubergine slices in a colander, sprinkle with salt and leave to drain while you prepare the other vegetables. Blanch the courgettes, asparagus spears (if using) and cauliflower florets in separate pans of boiling salted water for 2 minutes. Drain, refresh under cold water and dry well on kitchen paper. Rinse the aubergine slices and pat dry on kitchen paper.

Next make the batter. Put the chickpea or gram flour, coriander, 1 scant teaspoon salt and the curry powder into a large bowl. Gradually whisk in the oil, lemon juice and water until the batter is the consistency of thick cream. Leave to stand for 1 hour.

Heat good-quality oil to 180°C/350°F in a deep-fat fryer. Lightly whisk the batter and dip the vegetables in batches of 5 or 6, allowing the excess batter to drain back into the bowl.

Slip the vegetables carefully into the hot oil. Fry the pakoras for 2–3 minutes on each side, turning them with a slotted spoon. Drain them on kitchen paper and keep warm (uncovered) in a moderate oven while you cook the remainder. Always ensure the oil has returned to the correct temperature between batches. When all the vegetable fritters are ready, garnish with lemon wedges and fresh or deep-fried coriander or parsley. Serve at once with the yogurt raita.

Per serving: 299 kcals, 20g fat, 2g saturated fat, 19g carbohydrate, 0.29g sodium, 105mg calcium

Cucumber and yogurt raita

¼ medium-sized cucumber

½ tablespoon chopped onion

Salt and freshly ground black pepper

150ml (5fl oz) plain yogurt

½–1 tomato, diced

1 tablespoon chopped coriander or ½ tablespoon parsley and ½ tablespoon mint

½ teaspoon whole cumin seeds

Peel the cucumber if you prefer, cut in half lengthwise and remove the seeds. Cut into 5mm (¼in) dice. Put them in a bowl with the onion, sprinkle with ¼ teaspoon salt and allow to degorge for 5–10 minutes. Drain, and add to the yogurt, along with the diced tomato and chopped herbs. Heat the cumin seeds, crush lightly and add to the raita. Taste and adjust the seasoning if necessary. Chill before serving.

Per serving: 19 kcals, 1g fat, 0g saturated fat, 3g carbohydrate, 0.15g sodium, 55mg calcium

Chickpea, potato and spinach curry

Radha Patterson, co-owner (with Mary Maw) of the excellent
Belfast deli Cargoes, passed on this delicious veggie curry to us.
Feel free to add in a few extra vegetables if you like. **Serves 6-8**

225g (8oz) dried chickpeas, soaked overnight in cold water

5 tablespoons sunflower oil

275g (10oz) onions, chopped

2 fresh green chillies, deseeded and finely chopped

2 teaspoons grated fresh ginger

1 tablespoon cumin seeds

1 tablespoon paprika

2 tablespoons concentrated tomato purée

1 teaspoon ground fenugreek seeds

2 teaspoons ground turmeric

2 teaspoons ground cumin

750g (1lb 10oz) baby new potatoes or any other firm waxy potatoes

Salt and freshly ground black pepper

400g (14oz) tinned tomatoes, chopped

250g (8oz) spinach, destalked

2 tablespoons fresh coriander leaves, to garnish

Drain the chickpeas, cover with fresh cold water and bring to the boil. Reduce the heat and cook until tender, which can take from 30–60 minutes depending on the age and quality.

Meanwhile, heat 2 tablespoons of the oil in a wide, heavy-based saucepan and add the chopped onions and green chillies. Cook gently until the onions are soft but not coloured. Add the grated ginger and continue to cook for a further minute.

Dry-roast the cumin seeds and paprika in small pan. Remove from the heat and crush the cumin seeds using a pestle and mortar or a spice grinder. Add the spices to the cooked onion mixture and stir the contents of the pan.

Once the chickpeas are soft, remove from the heat and drain, reserving the cooking liquid. Add the drained chickpeas to the pan and stir around. Mix the tomato purée with 150ml (¼ pint) of the reserved hot chickpea cooking liquid in a small bowl. Add the ground fenugreek seeds and pour over the chickpeas. Simmer the contents of the pan for 5 minutes, taking care not to burn the fenugreek seeds.

In another heavy-based frying pan, heat the remaining sunflower oil and add the ground turmeric and cumin. When the oil is hot, add the potatoes and season with salt and freshly ground black pepper. Fry the potatoes on all sides until they are crispy and then add the contents of the pan to the chickpea mixture. Lastly, add the chopped tomatoes and 500ml (18fl oz) of the reserved chickpea cooking liquid. Bring the contents of the pan to the boil, cover and reduce the heat. Simmer gently for about 20–25 minutes or until the potatoes are tender.

Add the destalked spinach to the pan, adding a little extra chickpea cooking liquid if necessary. Cook over a medium heat, uncovered, for 3–5 minutes, or until the spinach has wilted. Taste and adjust the seasoning if necessary.

Sprinkle the top with coriander leaves and serve with gluten-free naan bread (see page 123) and plain boiled rice.

Per serving: 379 kcals, 14g fat, 2g saturated fat, 51g carbohydrate, 0.21g sodium, 228mg calcium

Crackling salmon with coriander

pesto *All kinds of fish – and meat – can be wrapped in rice paper. Keep a few packets in the cupboard and experiment. Use smaller rice wrappers (16cm/6½in) for a starter portion.* **Serves 4**

200–450g (7oz–1lb) wild or
organic salmon fillets – allow
110g (4oz) per person for a
main course or 50g (2oz) as
a starter: salmon is very rich
Rice paper wrappers (Bánh
Tráng), 23cm (9in) diameter

Coriander leaves
Coriander pesto (see recipe)
Salt and freshly ground black
pepper
Sunflower oil, for frying
To garnish
Lemon wedges
Coriander sprigs

Remove the skin of the salmon. Place the salmon fillet skin-side down on a board. Cut through the flesh down onto the skin at the tail end, with the knife at a 45° angle. Hold onto the skin and half push, half saw the flesh off the skin. If the knife is at the correct angle, there should be no waste.

Cut the salmon fillet into 4 pieces, each measuring approximately 7 x 5cm (3 x 2in) for a main course.

Fill a wide bowl with very hot water. Rice wrappers break easily, so handle them carefully. Dip one wrapper at a time into the hot water; it will soften in 5–10 seconds.

Remove the rice wrapper carefully, shake off excess moisture and place on a clean tea-towel. Be gentle with the softened wrappers as they can be easily torn.

Lay 2 coriander leaves in the centre of each wrapper.

Split 1 of the salmon pieces almost in half using a sharp knife, stopping about 2.5cm (1in) from the edge (so that the salmon piece opens out like a book).

Smear about 1 teaspoon coriander pesto onto the cut flesh, season with salt and freshly ground black pepper. Close over the salmon fillet and place it directly on top of the coriander leaves on the rice wrapper.

Fold the bottom of the wrapper over the salmon, then fold in the two adjacent sides. Fold it over again and press to seal, making a neat parcel.

Heat the sunflower oil in a heavy-based non-stick frying pan. Put the salmon parcel in the pan – presentation side down – and cook for about 4 minutes. Use a plastic fish slice to flip over and cook on the other side. The rice wrapper should be golden brown and crisp. If your salmon is a thick piece, you may prefer to finish cooking the parcels on a baking sheet in a preheated oven, 180°C/350°F/gas mark 4, for 5–10 minutes, to ensure the salmon is cooked through before the rice wrappers get too brown.

Transfer the crackling salmon to warm plates and serve immediately with a wedge of lemon and coriander sprigs to garnish. It is delicious served with a green salad and tiny new potatoes.

Per serving including coriander pesto: 455 kcals, 36g fat, 6g saturated fat, 6g carbohydrate, 0.2g sodium, 110mg calcium

Coriander pesto

50ml (2fl oz) light olive oil or
peanut oil
1 spring onion, white and
green parts, coarsely
chopped
1 garlic clove, coarsely
chopped
1 tablespoon pine nuts,
toasted

1½ teaspoons freshly
squeezed lemon or lime
juice
1 lightly packed cup coriander
sprigs with short stems
1 lightly packed cup flat
parsley sprigs, large stems
removed
Salt
Cayenne pepper

Mix everything except the seasoning in a blender. Add salt and a few pinches of cayenne, then purée until smooth. Taste and adjust the seasoning if necessary.

Crispy fish with tartare sauce

Almost any fish can be cooked this way, but watch that the fillet isn't too thick or it may be overcooked on the outside but underdone in the centre.

Serves 4 as a main course or 8 as a starter

4 mackerel, plaice or lemon sole, cleaned	Sunflower oil, for deep-frying
Seasoned rice flour	**To serve**
2 eggs, whisked with a little milk	Lemon wedges
Fresh white gluten-free breadcrumbs (see page 118)	Flat parsley sprigs
	Tartare sauce (see recipe)

Wash the fish, fillet carefully and dry on kitchen paper. Preheat the deep-fat fryer to 180°C/350°F. Coat each piece first in seasoned flour, then in egg and finally in crumbs. When the oil is hot, fry a few fillets at a time and drain on kitchen paper. Serve with a lemon wedge, parsley and tartare sauce.

Per serving as a main course: 606 kcals, 47g fat, 9g saturated fat, 9g carbohydrate, 0.3g sodium, 69mg calcium

Tartare sauce Serves 8–10

2 hard-boiled eggs and 2 raw egg yolks	Salt and freshly ground pepper
¼ teaspoon gluten-free Dijon mustard	1 teaspoon chopped capers
1–2 tbsp white wine vinegar	1 teaspoon chopped gherkins
350ml (12fl oz) sunflower or arachide oil	2 teaspoons chopped chives or spring onions
	2 teaspoons chopped parsley

Sieve the hard-boiled egg yolks into a bowl (reserving the whites). Mix in the raw egg yolks, mustard and 1 tablespoon wine vinegar. Whisk in the oil drop by drop, increasing the volume as the mixture thickens. When all the oil has been absorbed, add the capers, gherkins, chives or onions, and parsley. **Chop** the hard-boiled egg whites roughly and fold in. Season and add a little more vinegar or lemon juice if necessary.

Per serving: 400 kcals, 43g fat, 6g saturated fat, 0g carbohydrate, 0.15g sodium, 20mg calcium

Pan-grilled mackerel with watercress butter

Really fresh mackerel is sublime; you can cook it in many ways, but pan-grilled is great. Try pan-grilling other fish – grey mullet, turbot, hake and cod are particularly delicious. Serves 4

8 fillets of very fresh mackerel (allow 175g (6oz) fish per person for a main course, 75g (3oz) for a starter)	Watercress butter (see page 155)
	To serve
Seasoned rice flour	Lemon wedges
Small knob of butter	Flat parsley or watercress sprigs

First make the watercress butter and refrigerate.
Preheat the grill pan. Dip the fish fillets in the seasoned rice flour. Shake off the excess flour and then spread a little butter with a knife on the flesh side, as though you were buttering a slice of bread rather meanly. When the grill is quite hot but not smoking, place the fish fillets butter-side down on the grill; the fish should sizzle as soon as they touch the pan. Reduce the heat slightly and let them cook for 4–5 minutes on that side before turning them over. Continue to cook on the other side until crisp and golden.
Serve on hot plates with a wedge of lemon and some slices of watercress butter melting over them and a sprig of parsley or watercress.

Fillets of any small fish are delicious pan-grilled in this way. Fish under 900g (2lb), such as mackerel, herring and brown trout, can also be grilled whole on the pan. Fish over 900g (2lb) can be filleted first and then cut across into portions. Large fish 1.8–2.6kg (4–6lb) can also be grilled whole. Cook them for about 10–15 minutes on each side and then put in a hot oven for about another 15 minutes to finish cooking.

Per serving: 621 kcals, 53g fat, 21g saturated fat, 3g carbohydrate, 0.44g sodium, 36mg calcium

Ballyandreen fish pie with buttered leeks and garlic butter

Ballyandreen is a tiny cove near Ballymaloe. We often collect periwinkles and little mussels to add to the fish pie, but it is delicious without shellfish. **Serves 6**

600ml (1 pint) milk

1 small onion, sliced and 225g (8oz) onions, finely chopped

3–4 slices of carrot

3 black peppercorns

Small bay leaf

Sprig of thyme

25g (1oz) butter

225g (8oz) mushrooms, sliced

1.1kg (2½lb) mixed fillets of cod, haddock and salmon (wild or organic)

Salt and freshly ground black pepper

Gluten-free roux (see page 150)

2 tablespoons double cream (optional)

2 tablespoons freshly chopped parsley

1 tablespoon freshly chopped dill

Fluffy herbed potato (see recipe)

Garlic butter (see page 155)

For the buttered leeks

8 medium leeks, trimmed and sliced

50g (2oz) butter

2 tablespoons water (if needed)

Heat the milk in a pan with the sliced onion, carrot, peppercorns, bay leaf and thyme. Bring to the boil, simmer for 4–5 minutes, then remove from the heat and leave to infuse for 10 minutes.

Sweat the chopped onions in the butter over a low heat until soft but not coloured. Remove to a plate. Increase the heat, sauté the mushrooms in the same butter and season with salt and black pepper. Remove and add to the softened onion.

Cut the fish into 150g (5oz) chunks and season with salt and freshly ground black pepper. Put the fish into a wide sauté or frying pan, in a single layer, and cover with the strained milk. Cover and simmer gently until the fish is just cooked – no more than 3–4 minutes. Remove the fish with a slotted spoon and discard any bones or skin. Bring the milk to the boil and thicken with the gluten-free roux, add the cream (if using), herbs, fish, onions and mushrooms and taste for seasoning.

Prepare the leeks. Melt the butter in a heavy-based saucepan and, when it foams, toss in the sliced leeks so that they are coated in butter. Season with salt and freshly ground black pepper, cover with a paper lid and then the saucepan lid and reduce the heat. Cook very gently for about 10 minutes or until soft and moist, only adding water if they start to stick.

Transfer the fish mixture to a large pie dish and spread over the buttered leeks. Pipe the fluffy herbed potato on top. The pie may be prepared ahead to this point.

Preheat the oven to 180°C/350°F/gas mark 4. Cook the pie for 10–15 minutes if the filling and mashed potato are warm, or 30 minutes if you are reheating it from cold. Flash under the grill if you need to brown the top. Serve with garlic butter.

Per serving with leeks and potatoes: 759 kcals, 41g fat, 21g saturated fat, 48g carbohydrate, 0.68g sodium, 295mg calcium

Fluffy herbed potatoes

900g (2lb) unpeeled potatoes, preferably Golden Wonder

300ml (½ pint) creamy milk

1–2 egg whites or 1 whole egg and 1 egg white

Salt and freshly ground pepper

2 tablespoons freshly chopped herbs (parsley, chives, thyme or lemon balm)

25–50g (1–2oz) butter

Scrub the potatoes well, then put in a saucepan of cold water with a good pinch of salt and bring to the boil. When the potatoes are half cooked (after about 15 minutes), strain off two-thirds of the water, replace the lid, put on a low heat and allow the potatoes to steam until fully cooked. Peel immediately by just pulling off the skins and mash while hot. (For a large quantity, put the potatoes into a mixer bowl and beat until smooth.) Bring the milk to the boil. Beat the egg whites into the hot mashed potatoes and add enough boiling milk to mix to a fluffy consistency. Add the herbs and then beat in the butter and seasoning to your taste.

Fishcakes with parsley or garlic butter

These tasty fish cakes are a good way to use up any leftover cooked fish. You could also served them with Tartare Sauce (see page 92) or perhaps a spicy salsa. **Serves 8**

Garlic butter (see page 155)
50g (2oz) butter
225g (8oz) onions, finely chopped
225g (8oz) mashed potato
450g (1lb) leftover cooked fish, e.g. salmon (wild or organic), cod, haddock, hake (a little smoked fish, say haddock or mackerel is good), flaked
2 tablespoons gluten-free nam pla (fish sauce; optional)

1 egg, preferably free range, lightly beaten
2 tablespoons chopped parsley
Salt and freshly ground black pepper
Seasoned rice flour
1–2 eggs, preferably free range, lightly beaten
Fresh gluten-free breadcrumbs (see page 118)
Clarified butter (see page 112) or a mixture of butter and oil, for frying

First make the garlic butter and refrigerate.

Melt the butter in a saucepan, toss in the onions, cover and sweat over a gentle heat for 4–5 minutes, until soft but not coloured. Scrape the contents of the pan into a bowl, add the mashed potato, flaked cooked fish, nam pla (if using), 1 lightly beaten egg and the parsley. Season with salt and freshly ground black pepper. Taste and adjust the seasoning if necessary.

Shape the mixture into 16 fishcakes. Coat them first in seasoned rice flour, then in beaten egg and finally in gluten-free breadcrumbs. Chill until needed, then cook on a medium heat in clarified butter until golden brown on both sides. Alternatively, the fishcakes can be placed on a baking sheet and cooked in a preheated oven, 180°C/350°F/gas mark 4, for about 25 minutes, turning half way through, until they are piping hot and golden brown.

Serve two fishcakes per person on hot plates with a little slice of the garlic butter melting on top of each one accompanied with Tomato Fondue (see page 154) and a green salad.

Per serving, without garlic butter: 287 kcals, 19g fat, 9g saturated fat, 14g carbohydrate, 0.28g sodium, 42mg calcium

Thai fishcakes with thai dipping sauce

Haddock, hake or cod also work beautifully in this recipe. Serve with crisp lettuce leaves, lots of fresh herbs and a Thai dipping sauce. **Serves 4–5**

1 onion, finely chopped
4 spring onions, finely chopped
2–3 small red chillies, finely chopped
2 lemongrass stalks, outer leaves removed, very finely chopped
2.5cm (1in) piece fresh ginger, grated
3 garlic cloves, crushed with a little salt
Sunflower oil, for frying

500g (1lb) salmon fillet (wild or organic), skinned
2 kaffir lime leaves, finely shredded
3 tablespoons fresh chopped coriander
1 egg white, preferably free range
75g (3oz) rice flour
Salt and freshly ground black pepper
Thai Dipping Sauce (see page 60)

Mix the onion, spring onions, chillies, lemongrass, grated ginger and crushed garlic. Heat 2 tablespoons sunflower oil in a pan and cook this mixture for 2–3 minutes until soft. Allow to cool.

Chop the salmon into 5mm (¼in) dice or whiz in a food-processor for a few seconds. Combine the cooled onion mixture, salmon, kaffir lime leaves, coriander, egg white and rice flour. Season the mixture with salt and freshly ground black pepper.

Cook a little of the mixture in the sunflower oil in a hot frying pan, taste for seasoning and adjust if necessary. Shape into 8–10 small rounds and flatten to 1.5cm (¾in) thick. At this point the raw fishcakes may be frozen successfully if they are placed between sheets of parchment paper and covered with clingfilm. Allow to defrost thoroughly before cooking. Heat a little sunflower oil in a frying pan to a medium heat. Fry the fishcakes until golden brown on each side and cooked through. Serve with Thai Dipping Sauce, Thai Rice Noodle Salad (see page 52) and a fresh green salad.

Per serving: 401 kcals, 24g fat, 4g saturated fat, 19g carbohydrate, 0.13g sodium, 48mg calcium

Spicy chicken goujons

This is the way Darina's son Isaac Allen, Chef of the Crawford Gallery Café in Cork, prepares chicken goujons. They are irresistible eaten freshly fried with the hot and sweet sauce. **Serves 4**

4 skinless and boneless chicken
  breasts, preferably free range
For the spicy seasoned flour
150g (5oz) rice flour
3 tablespoons sesame seeds
½ tablespoon gluten-free
  curry powder
¼ teaspoon cayenne pepper

Salt and ground black pepper
Fire and Brimstone Sauce
  (see recipe)
Rocket leaves
Dressing of extra virgin olive
  oil and balsamic vinegar
Oil, for deep frying
A little milk

Cut the chicken breasts into 5mm (¼in) thick strips.

Mix the ingredients together for the spicy seasoned flour and place in a wide pie dish.

Next, make the Fire and Brimstone Sauce.

Just before serving, heat the oil in a deep-fat fryer to 200°C/400°F. Toss a few pieces of chicken in milk, then in the spicy flour. Deep-fry a few pieces at a time.

Toss the rocket leaves with the dressing. Pile a handful of rocket salad on plates and top with a serving of chicken goujons. Drizzle with Fire and Brimstone Sauce and serve.

Per serving: 331 kcals, 7g fat, 1g saturated fat, 31g carbohydrate, 0.23g sodium, 89mg calcium

Fire and brimstone sauce *Serves 8–10*

2–4 red chillies
4 garlic cloves, crushed
225g (8oz) apricot jam

5 tablespoons white wine
  vinegar
Good pinch of salt

Deseed and roughly chop the chillies, then whiz all the ingredients in a food processor. This sauce keeps for up to 2 weeks in a covered jar in the fridge.

Per serving: 85 kcals, 0g fat, 0g saturated fat, 22g carbohydrate, 0.11g sodium, 5mg calcium

Crispy basil and pine nut chicken sandwich

Not a sandwich in the normal sense – the chicken breast has a filling of garlicky basil butter and a coating of crispy gluten-free crumbs. **Serves 4**

4 chicken breasts, preferably free range

For the filling

2 tablespoons pine nuts

Good handful of fresh basil leaves

50g (2oz) Parmesan, freshly grated

2 garlic cloves, finely chopped

50g (2oz) butter, softened

Salt and freshly ground black pepper

For the crispy coating

Seasoned rice flour, for dipping

2 eggs, preferably free range, lightly beaten

200g (7oz) gluten-free breadcrumbs (see page 118)

25g (1oz) pine nuts, finely chopped

Preheat the oven to 180°C/350°F/gas mark 4. Spread the pine nuts for the filling on a baking tray and toast for about 8 minutes. Watch carefully as they can easily burn round the edges. Leave to cool.

To make the filling, place the basil, toasted pine nuts, Parmesan cheese, garlic and soft butter into the bowl of a food-processor. Add salt and freshly ground black pepper and whiz using the pulse button, scraping down the sides occasionally. The butter is now ready to use or you can form it into a log, wrap it in parchment paper and freeze it for use at a later date.

Prepare the chicken by first detaching the little fillet from the chicken breast. Set it aside. Carefully slit the chicken breast down the side and open out. Season with salt and freshly ground black pepper and smear about 1 tablespoon of the flavoured butter on one side of the chicken breast.

Place the little detached fillet on top of the butter and fold over the other side of the chicken breast. Press well to seal and mould the chicken into a thick log shape. Repeat with the remaining breasts.

Dip each stuffed chicken breast first in seasoned rice flour, then into the beaten eggs, then into the breadcrumbs and then into the finely chopped pine nuts. This process can be repeated if you want a thicker crumb.

Place the chicken breasts in an ovenproof gratin dish and bake in the oven for approximately 35–40 minutes – depending on their thickness. Ensure they are cooked through by carefully cutting one open at an angle to minimise the loss of the lovely garlicky basil butter, which will ooze out. The chicken juices should run clear.

Serve immediately on a bed of rice noodles (try the Vietnamese Noodle Salad recipe on page 52) or with roast potatoes and a lovely green salad. The sandwich is also delicious with pasta.

Per serving: 547 kcals, 30g fat, 12g saturated fat, 22g carbohydrate, 0.65g sodium, 228mg calcium

Chicken, mushroom and tarragon pie

Chicken pot pies are comfort food at its very best, and now coeliacs can also enjoy this perennial favourite. Seek out free-range organic chicken breasts if at all possible. **Serves 6**

1.2 litres (2 pints) homemade chicken stock (see page 153)

700g (1½lb) chicken breasts preferably free range and organic

1 quantity Rosemary's savoury pastry (see page 150)

2 quantities Mushroom à la crème (see page 151), made without the parsley and chives

1 tablespoon finely chopped French tarragon

Salt and freshly ground black pepper

Egg wash

Round pie dish or oval ovenproof dish, 23cm (9in) diameter, sides 4cm (1¼in) high

Bring the chicken stock to the boil in a sauté pan just large enough to accommodate the chicken breasts in one layer. Simmer gently for 5–7 minutes, depending on the size. Turn off the heat, cover and allow the chicken to cool in the liquid. Remove with a slotted spoon. Reserve the chicken stock. Make the pastry in the usual way. Cover and refrigerate.

Meanwhile make double the recipe for Mushroom à la Crème and stir in the finely chopped tarragon. Allow the sauce to reduce for a few minutes. Add 175–225ml (6–8fl oz) of the reserved chicken stock to the sauce – this will make the pie filling nice and juicy.

Cut the chicken into 2.5cm (1½in) slices and add to the mushroom mixture. (If you are preparing the pie in advance, cool the chicken first.) Taste and season with salt and freshly ground black pepper.

Preheat the oven to 180°C/350°F/gas mark 4.

Fill the pie dish with the chicken mixture. Roll the pastry out thinly, 3–5mm (⅛–¼in) thick. Brush the edge of the pie dish with water and stick a narrow band of pastry around the edge. Egg wash the top of the pastry edge, then cut out the pastry lid. Trim the edges and pinch the two layers of pastry tightly together to seal.

Brush the pastry lid with egg wash and roll out the trimmings to make pastry leaves to decorate the top of the pie. Brush the decorations with egg wash. Make a hole in the centre for the steam to escape, then bake in the oven for 45 minutes until the pastry is golden brown and the filling is hot. A fluffy potato topping (see page 93) instead of pastry is deliciously comforting.

Serve with a green salad.

Per serving: 724 kcals, 45g fat, 27g saturated fat, 42g carbohydrate, 0.96g sodium, 115mg calcium

Thai chicken stir-fry with pak choi

Stir-fries are a brilliant way to produce tasty, healthy meals fast. And cooking in one pan saves on washing up! For a change, try spinach and tiger prawns instead of pak choi and chicken. **Serves 4**

110g (4oz) gluten-free flat rice noodles

225g (8oz) pak choi

2 large red chillies, deseeded and sliced thinly at an angle

10 spring onions, thinly sliced at an angle

1 tablespoon fresh grated ginger

1 teaspoon chopped garlic

150g (5oz) mushrooms, thinly sliced

500g (1lb 2oz) chicken breasts, preferably free range and organic, thinly sliced

Vegetable oil, for frying

1 tablespoon cornflour

125ml (4fl oz) homemade chicken stock (see page 153)

1 red pepper, quartered, deseeded and cut into thin strips across (not lengthwise)

75g (3oz) plain cashew nuts

2 tablespoons gluten-free Japanese tamari soy sauce

2 tablespoons gluten-free nam pla (fish sauce)

Few drops of toasted sesame oil (optional)

Fresh coriander leaves, to garnish

Soak the rice noodles in a bowl of very hot water for 15–20 minutes or until soft. Drain in a colander.

Remove the stem sections of the pak choi and cut into lengths measuring about 2.5cm (1in). Cut the leafy part into squares measuring 2.5cm (1in) and keep separate from the stem sections. Set aside until required.

Prepare all the vegetables and chicken before you start to cook.

Heat a wok or large, heavy-based frying pan over a high heat until it smokes, add 2 tablespoons oil and reheat. Add the chillies, spring onions, ginger and garlic and toss around. Add the mushrooms and cook over a high heat, continuing to stir and fry for 2 minutes until the mushrooms wilt. Remove from the wok and set aside.

Heat another tablespoon of oil in the wok if necessary, and add the sliced chicken. Cook, stirring continuously, for a further 3–4 minutes or until golden.

Mix the cornflour with the cold chicken stock and set aside.

Add the red pepper, cashew nuts, tamari soy sauce and nam pla sauce to the wok. Stir for 1 minute. Return the onion mixture to the pan, toss well and add the drained flat rice noodles. Toss well again. Pour the slaked cornflour into the contents of the wok and stir. Allow the sauce to thicken slightly, and then toss in the pak choi stalks. Cook quickly over a high heat for a minute before adding the leafy part of the pak choi. Cook for another minute or two until the pak choi wilts and the noodles heat through. If you wish, add a few drops of toasted sesame oil. Serve immediately on hot plates, garnished with coriander leaves.

Per serving: 450 kcals, 17g fat, 2g saturated fat, 39g carbohydrate, 1.33g sodium, 74mg calcium

Chicken and broccoli gratin

This is one of those dishes that can be mouth-watering or a complete disaster. Its success depends on the broccoli being carefully cooked so that it is bright green and just tender. **Serves 6**

1 x 1.6kg (3½lb) chicken, preferably free range
2 carrots, sliced
2 onions, sliced
Sprig each of thyme and tarragon
Few peppercorns
300ml (½ pint) homemade chicken stock (see page 153)
Salt and freshly ground black pepper
450g (1lb) broccoli florets
110g (4oz) mushrooms, sliced
Scrap of butter

175ml (6fl oz) milk
150ml (5fl oz) single cream
2 teaspoons chopped tarragon or annual marjoram
Gluten-free roux (see page 150)
25g (1oz) buttered gluten-free crumbs (see recipe)
25g (1oz) mature Cheddar cheese, grated

Lasagne dish, 25 x 20cm (10 x 8 in)

Put the chicken into a large saucepan or flameproof casserole with the carrots and onions and add a sprig of thyme and tarragon and a few peppercorns. Pour in the stock, bring to the boil, cover and simmer for 1–1½ hours or until the chicken is tender.

Meanwhile bring 600ml (1 pint) water with 1½ teaspoons salt to a fast boil. Cook the broccoli florets, uncovered, in the boiling salted water until *al dente*. Drain and refresh under cold water, then set aside.

Sauté the mushrooms in the butter in a hot pan, season with salt and freshly ground pepper, then set aside too.

When the chicken is cooked, remove the meat from one side and carve into bite-sized pieces. (Keep the remainder for another recipe or double the rest of the ingredients.)

Strain and degrease the cooking liquid, add the milk and cream, bring to the boil, add the chopped tarragon or annual marjoram, simmer for a few minutes, thicken to a light coating consistency with the gluten-free roux, then add the chicken to the sauce. Season with salt and freshly ground black pepper.

Preheat the oven to 180°C/350°F/gas mark 4 and butter an ovenproof lasagne dish. Put a layer of broccoli on the base, scatter the mushrooms on top and cover with the creamy chicken mixture.

Mix the buttered gluten-free breadcrumbs with the grated cheese and sprinkle over the surface. Reheat in the oven for 15–20 minutes, then flash under the grill until the top is crunchy and golden. Serve immediately.

Per serving: 517 kcals, 33g fat, 18g saturated fat, 25g carbohydrate, 0.45g sodium, 183mg calcium

Buttered gluten-free crumbs

Melt 15g (½oz) butter, remove from the heat and stir in 25g (1oz) gluten-free breadcrumbs (see page 118). Allow to cool.

Old-fashioned roast turkey with fresh herb stuffing
A turkey wouldn't be the same without stuffing, especially at Christmas. You can cook a chicken this way, but use a quarter of the stuffing. **Serves 10–12**

1 x 4.5–5.5kg (10–12lb) turkey with neck and giblets, preferably free range and organic

Gluten-free roux (see page 150; optional)

For the fresh herb stuffing

350g (12oz) onions, chopped

175g (6oz) butter

400–450g (14oz–1lb) gluten-free breadcrumbs (see page 118)

50g (2oz) fresh herbs, e.g. parsley, thyme, chives, marjoram, savory, lemon balm, chopped

Salt and freshly ground black pepper

For the stock

Neck, gizzard, heart, wishbone and wingtips of the turkey

2 carrots, sliced

2 onions, sliced

1 celery stick

Bouquet garni

3–4 peppercorns

For basting the turkey

225g (8oz) butter

Large square of muslin (optional)

To garnish

Sprigs of fresh flat parsley or watercress

To serve

Gluten-free cranberry sauce

Gluten-free bread sauce

Remove the wishbone from the neck end of the turkey, for ease of carving later. Make a turkey stock by covering the neck, gizzard, heart, wishbone, wingtips, vegetables and bouquet garni with cold water (keep the liver for smooth turkey liver pâté). Bring to the boil and simmer for about 3 hours while the turkey is being prepared and cooked.

To make the fresh herb stuffing, sweat the onions gently in the butter for about 10 minutes, until soft, then stir in the gluten-free crumbs, herbs and a little salt and pepper to taste. Allow it to get quite cold. If necessary, wash and dry the cavity of the bird, then season and half-fill with the cold stuffing. Put the remainder of the stuffing into the crop at the neck end.

Preheat the oven to 180°C/350°F/gas mark 4.

Weigh the turkey and calculate the cooking time. Allow approximately 15 minutes per 450g (1lb) and 15 minutes over.

Melt 4 teaspoons of the basting butter and soak a large piece of good-quality muslin in it; cover the turkey completely with the muslin and roast in the oven for 3–3½ hours. There is no need to baste it because of the butter-soaked muslin. The turkey browns beautifully, but if you like it even browner, remove the muslin 10 minutes before the end of the cooking time. Alternatively, smear the breast, legs and crop well with soft butter and season with salt and freshly ground black pepper. If the turkey is not covered with butter-soaked muslin, it is a good idea to cover the whole dish with aluminium foil. However, your turkey will then be semi-steamed, not roasted, in the traditional sense of the word.

Test whether the turkey is cooked by pricking the thickest part at the base of the thigh and examine the juices: they should be clear. Remove the turkey to a carving dish, keep it warm and allow it to rest while you make the gravy.

To make the gravy, spoon off the surplus fat from the roasting pan. Deglaze the pan juices with fat-free stock from the giblets and bones. Use a whisk to stir and scrape the base to dissolve the caramelised meat juices from the roasting pan. Boil it up well, season and thicken with a little gluten-free roux if you like. Taste and adjust the seasoning if necessary. Serve in a hot gravy boat.

If possible, present the turkey on your largest serving dish, surrounded by crispy roast potatoes, and garnished with large sprigs of parsley or watercress and maybe a sprig of holly, (make sure no one eats the berries).

Serve with gluten-free cranberry sauce and gluten-free bread sauce.

Per serving: 621 kcals, 34g fat, 17g saturated fat, 18g carbohydrate, 0.55g sodium, 74mg calcium

Lamburgers with tsatsiki, fresh mint chutney and poppadoms

People are familiar with hamburgers, but why not use lamb meat occasionally? Get your butcher to mince some lamb shoulder. **Serves 6**

225g (8oz) onions, finely chopped

50g (2oz) butter or 2 tablespoons extra virgin olive oil

1kg (2¼lb) minced shoulder of lamb

2 teaspoons coriander seeds, toasted and ground

2 teaspoons cumin seeds, toasted and ground

2 eggs, preferably free range, lightly beaten

Salt and freshly ground black pepper

To serve

4 poppadoms – ensure they are gluten-free

Sunflower oil

Tsatsiki (see page 154)

Fresh Mint Chutney (see page 154)

Sweat the finely chopped onions gently in the butter or olive oil until soft but not coloured. Leave to cool. Add them to the minced lamb with the ground spices. Add the lightly beaten eggs and mix well. Season with salt and freshly ground black pepper. Shape into 12 burger or patty shapes and refrigerate until required.

Cook the burgers on a hot grill or in a frying pan for about 4 minutes on each side, or according to your taste.

Deep-fry the poppadoms, or brush with oil and place under a hot grill for a few seconds only until they puff up.

Serve the lamburgers with poppadoms, tsatsiki and fresh mint chutney.

Per serving including poppadoms, tsatsiki and mint chutney:
614 kcals, 41g fat, 21g saturated fat, 20g carbohydrate, 0.52g sodium, 227mg calcium

Lamb korma

Radha Patterson, a native of Delhi in India, gave us this recipe. Radha co-owns (with Mary Maw) the gorgeous deli in Belfast called Cargoes, where Rosemary worked for some time. **Serves 8**

1.1kg (2½lb) boneless lamb (leg or shoulder is perfect)
2 tablespoons whole coriander seeds
2 tablespoons paprika
2 teaspoons ground turmeric
4 tablespoons vegetable oil
225g (8oz) onions, finely chopped
10 cardamom pods
1 cinnamon stick
6 black peppercorns
6 cloves
2 teaspoons fresh grated ginger
4 garlic cloves, crushed with a little sea salt
25g (1oz) clarified butter (see page 112)
500ml (18fl oz) natural yogurt
225ml (8fl oz) single cream
75g (3oz) ground almonds

Cut the lamb into 4cm (1½in) cubes and refrigerate.

Dry-roast the coriander seeds in a pan over a medium heat for 1–2 minutes. Remove from the heat and crush coarsely using a pestle and mortar or spice grinder. Mix the ground coriander with the paprika and turmeric. Set aside.

Heat the oil in a large lidded saucepan, add the onions and sauté over a medium heat until they are pale golden. Transfer to a plate. In the same pan, add the cardamon pods, cinnamon stick, black peppercorns and cloves and fry gently to flavour the oil. Then carefully remove the whole spices with a slotted spoon and discard.

Return the onions to the pan and add the grated ginger and crushed garlic. Add the ground coriander, turmeric and paprika and cook for 1–2 minutes. Transfer to a plate.

In the same pan, heat the clarified butter and brown the meat over a high heat. Return the onions and spice mixture to the pot and mix through the browned lamb. Add the natural yogurt, a tablespoon at a time, stirring well to combine.

Add a little water, just enough to cover the lamb. Be careful, though, not to add too much water – you don't want the sauce to be too runny. (If, however, you are making this curry in advance to reheat later, the sauce will thicken slightly, so you will need to add a little extra water to achieve the desired consistency.) Stir the contents of the saucepan and cover it with a lid.

Simmer gently on top of the stove or, better still, in the oven, at 160°C/325°F/gas mark 3 for about 1 hour or until the meat is cooked. When the lamb is tender, stir in the cream and the ground almonds and simmer gently until heated through.

Serve with gluten-free naan bread (see page 123) and plain boiled rice.

Per serving: 504 kcals, 37g fat, 15g saturated fat, 11g carbohydrate, 0.15g sodium, 195mg calcium

Beefburgers with portobello mushrooms and marjoram butter

For great burgers, always use the beef on the day it is minced. A tiny amount of fat in it makes the burgers sweet and juicy. **Serves 4-6**

10g (½oz) butter
50g (2oz) onions, chopped
450g (1lb) freshly minced beef (flank, chump or shin would be perfect)
½ teaspoon fresh thyme leaves
½ teaspoon finely chopped flat parsley
1 small egg, preferably free range, beaten (optional)

Salt and freshly ground black pepper
Pork caul fat (optional)
Olive oil
4–6 Portobello mushrooms
Extra virgin olive oil
1 garlic clove, sliced
2–3 gluten-free burger buns

For the marjoram butter
50g (2oz) butter
2 tablespoons chopped marjoram

Preheat the oven to 200°C/400°F/gas mark 6.

Melt the butter in a saucepan and toss in the chopped onions. Sweat until soft but not coloured, then allow to cool.

Meanwhile mix the mince with the herbs and beaten egg (if using; it is not essential, but the addition of egg helps to bind the burgers and increases the food value), season with salt and freshly ground black pepper, add the onions and mix well. Fry off a tiny bit in a pan to check the seasoning and adjust if necessary. Then shape into 4–6 burgers. Wrap each one loosely in caul fat (if using) to allow for contraction during cooking.

Make the marjoram butter. Cream the butter, add the marjoram and lots of freshly ground pepper. Form into a roll, wrap in parchment paper and aluminium foil and chill.

Remove the stalks from the Portobello mushrooms and discard. Put the mushrooms in a roasting tin. Drizzle with extra virgin olive oil, season with salt and freshly ground black pepper and add a few thin slivers of garlic. Cook in the oven for 10–15 minutes or until soft, tender and juicy.

Preheat the grill pan. When hot, cook the burgers for about 4 minutes on each side, or to your taste. If the beefburgers are being cooked in batches, ensure you wash and dry the pan between batches.

Split the gluten-free buns in half. Put one half on a warm plate and top with a burger and a portobello mushroom. Serve immediately with a slice of marjoram butter melting over the mushroom.

Per serving: 463 kcals, 31g fat, 15g saturated fat, 15g carbohydrate, 0.48g sodium, 90mg calcium

Italian beef stew

This makes a rich and gutsy stew – just the thing to tuck into on a chilly winter's evening. Serve it with potatoes or rice noodles and a good green salad.

Serves 6–8

- 1.3kg (3lb) well-hung stewing beef or lean flank
- 3 tablespoons extra virgin olive oil
- 275g (10oz) onions, sliced
- 2 large carrots, cut into 1cm (½in) slices
- 1 heaped tablespoon potato flour
- 150ml (¼ pint) red wine
- 150ml (¼ pint) homemade beef stock (see page 152)
- 225ml (8fl oz) homemade tomato purée (see recipe)
- Salt and freshly ground black pepper
- 150g (5oz) mushrooms, sliced
- 2 tablespoons chopped parsley
- 12–16 black or green olives (optional)

Preheat the oven to 160°C/325°F/gas mark 3.

Trim the meat of any excess fat, then cut into 4cm (1½in) cubes.

Heat 1 tablespoon of the oil in a flameproof casserole and sweat the sliced onions and carrots over a low heat with the lid on for 10 minutes.

Heat a little more oil in a frying pan until almost smoking. Sear the meat on all sides, reduce the heat, stir in the potato flour and cook for 1 minute. Mix together the wine, gluten-free beef stock and tomato purée and add gradually to the casserole.

Season with salt and freshly ground black pepper. Cover and cook in the oven for 2½–3 hours.

Meanwhile heat another tablespoon of oil and sauté the mushrooms. Add, with the parsley, to the casserole about 30 minutes before the end of cooking. Add the olives (if using) 5 minutes before the end of cooking.

Per serving: 452 kcals, 17g fat, 6g saturated fat, 13g carbohydrate, 0.31g sodium, 52mg calcium

Tomato purée

Tomato purée is one of the best ways of preserving the flavour of ripe summer tomatoes for winter. Use for soups, stews, casseroles, etc.

- 900g (2lb) very ripe tomatoes
- 1 small onion, chopped
- 1 teaspoon sugar
- Good pinch each of salt and freshly ground black pepper

Cut the tomatoes into quarters and put into a stainless-steel saucepan with the onion, sugar, salt and freshly ground black pepper. Cook on a gentle heat until the tomatoes are soft (no water is needed). Put through the fine blade of the mouli-legume or a nylon sieve. Allow to get cold, then refrigerate or freeze in small batches.

Per recipe: 223 kcals, 3g fat, 0g saturated fat, 44g carbohydrate, 0.88g sodium, 98mg calcium

Meatballs with tomato and caper sauce

Gutsy flavourful meatballs in a rich tomato sauce. If you hate capers with a passion, simply leave them out — the meal will still be delicious. **Serves 6**

For the meatballs
6 tablespoons extra virgin olive oil

150g (5oz) onions, finely chopped

1 garlic clove, crushed

900g (2lb) freshly minced beef, extra lean if you prefer

1 tablespoon capers

50g (2oz) Parmesan cheese, freshly grated

2 tablespoons fresh chopped, mixed thyme and marjoram

1 egg, preferably free range, beaten

Salt and freshly ground pepper

For the tomato and caper sauce
2 tablespoons capers

1 tablespoon extra virgin olive oil

125g (4oz) onions, sliced

1 garlic clove, crushed

150ml (5fl oz) dry white wine

2½ x 400g (14oz) tins of tomatoes

Sugar

150g (5oz) ball of buffalo mozzarella cheese

Basil leaves

To make the meatballs, heat 2 tablespoons of oil in a heavy stainless-steel saucepan over a gentle heat and add the onions and garlic. Cover the pan and sweat for 4 minutes. Leave the mixture to cool.

Mix the minced beef with the cold sweated onion and garlic in a large bowl. Rinse the capers in cold running water, dry on kitchen paper and roughly chop. Add the capers, grated Parmesan, herbs and beaten egg to the bowl. Season the mixture with salt and pepper and stir to combine.

Fry off a tiny bit to check the seasoning and adjust if necessary. Divide the mixture into 6 large or 12 small portions and shape each one into a round ball. Cover the meatballs and refrigerate until required.

Meanwhile make the tomato and caper sauce. Rinse the capers in cold running water and dry on kitchen paper

Heat the oil in a stainless-steel saucepan. Add the sliced onions and crushed garlic, toss until coated, cover and sweat on a low heat until soft but not coloured. Remove and leave to cool.

Add the wine and continue to cook until the wine is almost fully absorbed. Now stir in the capers. Slice the tinned tomatoes and add with all the juice to the onion mixture. Season with salt, freshly ground black pepper and sugar. Cook, uncovered, for about 30 minutes or until the tomatoes soften.

Meanwhile preheat the oven to 180°C/350°F/gas mark 4.

Preheat a cast-iron casserole. Add the remaining 4 tablespoons of oil and fry the meatballs (in batches if necessary) until they are brown all over. Be careful not to break them up.

Reduce the heat and pour over the tomato and caper sauce.

Top the meatballs with torn buffalo mozzarella and basil leaves.

Place the casserole in the oven for about 20 minutes until the meatballs are cooked and the mozzarella has partially melted.

Serve with gluten-free pasta and a good green salad.

Per serving using extra-lean mince: 811 kcals, 33g fat, 13g saturated fat, 73g carbohydrate, 0.88g sodium, 345mg calcium

Peppered roast beef, gravy, yorkshire pudding and horseradish

sauce *For flavour buy beef on the bone. Order ahead for well-hung, preferably days-aged meat.* **Serves 10**

1.8kg (4lb) sirloin of beef, well
   hung
Extra virgin olive oil
25–50g (1–2oz) black
   peppercorns, cracked
Sea salt
Sprigs of rosemary, watercress
   or flat parsley, to garnish
Gluten-free Yorkshire pudding
   (see page 148)
Horseradish sauce (see recipe)

For the gravy
425–600ml (¾–1 pint)
   homemade beef stock
   (see page 152)
Dash of red wine (optional)
Salt and freshly ground black
   pepper
Gluten-free roux (see page
   150; optional)

An hour or so before you plan to cook the meat, score the fat lightly, brush the surface of the meat with olive oil and coat with freshly cracked black pepper.

Preheat the oven to 250°C/475°F/gas mark 9. Place the meat in a roasting tin, fat-side up, sprinkle with sea salt and put into the fully heated oven. Roast for 15 minutes, then reduce the temperature to 180°C/350°F/gas mark 4. As the fat renders down it will baste the meat. Calculate the cooking time per 450g (1lb) and roast until the beef is cooked to your taste.

Make the batter for the Yorkshire pudding and leave to rest for about 1 hour. Make the horseradish sauce, cover and refrigerate.

Test the meat by pressing a lean surface: if the flesh springs back readily and feels quite soft, it is rare. Alternatively use a meat thermometer, but do not let it touch a bone, otherwise the reading will be inaccurate. (Beef is rare at an internal temperature of 60°C/140°F, medium at 70°C/158°F and well done at 75°C/167°F.)

When the meat is cooked, allow to rest on a plate in a warm oven for 15–30 minutes before carving, depending on the size of the roast. The internal temperature will continue to rise as much as 2–3°C/4–6°F, so remove the roast from the oven while it is still slightly less done than you would like.

Increase the oven to 230°C/450°F/gas mark 8.

Degrease the roasting tin, reserving the beef fat for roasting potatoes and cooking the Yorkshire pudding. Bake the Yorkshire puddings for 20 minutes.

Pour the beef stock into the roasting tin, put back on the heat and bring to the boil, and add a dash of red wine if you wish. Use a whisk to ensure that all the caramelized meat juices on the tin are dissolved. Season with salt and freshly ground black pepper and thicken with a tiny scrap of gluten-free roux if you wish. Taste and strain into a hot sauceboat.

Transfer the meat to a hot carving dish, adding any meat juices to the gravy. Cut the meat into slices about 3mm (⅛in) thick with a sharp carving knife. Serve on hot plates with a little gravy, Yorkshire pudding and roasted red onions.

Serve the horseradish sauce separately.

Per serving (roast beef and gravy only): 376 kcals, 22g fat, 9g saturated fat, 2g carbohydrate, 0.23g sodium, 28mg calcium

Horseradish sauce

1½–3 tablespoons scrubbed,
   peeled and grated
   horseradish root
1 teaspoon wine vinegar
1 teaspoon lemon juice
¼ teaspoon gluten-free mustard

¼ teaspoon salt
Freshly ground black pepper
1 teaspoon sugar
250ml (9fl oz) whipping
   cream, whipped into soft
   peaks

Put the grated horseradish into a bowl with the vinegar, lemon juice, mustard, salt, pepper and sugar. Fold in the softly whipped cream, but do not overmix or it will curdle. It keeps for 2–3 days, but cover it tightly so it does not pick up other flavours in the refrigerator.

Per serving: 61 kcals, 6g fat, 4g saturated fat, 1g carbohydrate, 0.06g sodium, 13mg calcium

Crispy bacon and mushroom cakes

Gluten-free chorizo sausage gives a gorgeous hot and spicy flavour and can be used instead of or as well as the bacon. The cakes can be prepared in advance and simply served with salad. **Makes** 10

25g (1oz) butter

110g (4oz) onions, finely chopped

175g (6oz) mushrooms, chopped

Extra virgin olive oil (optional)

175g (6oz) smoked streaky bacon, rind removed, cut into 1cm (½in) dice

350g (12oz) cooked mashed potatoes

1 egg yolk and 1–2 eggs, lightly beaten, preferably free range

2 tablespoons fresh chopped chives

1 tablespoon fresh chopped parsley

Salt and freshly ground black pepper

Seasoned rice flour

Fresh gluten-free breadcrumbs (see page 118)

Clarified butter (see recipe) or a mixture of butter and oil, for frying

Melt the butter in a heavy-based saucepan, toss in the onions, cover and sweat over a low heat for 4–5 minutes until soft but not coloured. Increase the heat and add the chopped mushrooms. Cook the mushrooms until they are wilted and all the moisture has been reabsorbed. Reduce the heat, add a little extra virgin olive oil if necessary, stir in the diced smoked streaky bacon and cook until crisp and golden.

Scrape the contents of the pan into a bowl, add the mashed potatoes, egg yolk and chopped herbs. Taste for seasoning and adjust if necessary. Take care with the seasoning as the bacon may be salty.

Form the mixture into 10 rounds. Coat the coats first in seasoned rice flour, then in beaten egg and finally in gluten-free breadcrumbs. Chill until required.

Cook the cakes in a heavy-based non-stick frying pan over a medium heat in clarified butter or butter and oil until golden on both sides. Alternatively, place them on a baking sheet and bake in a preheated oven, 180°C/350°F/gas mark 4, for about 25 minutes, turning halfway through cooking until they are piping hot, golden and crispy.

Serve on hot plates with a green salad.

Per serving: 195 kcals, 14g fat, 7g saturated fat, 12g carbohydrate, 0.35g sodium, 23mg calcium

Clarified butter

Melt 225g (8oz) butter gently in a saucepan or in the oven. Allow to stand for a few minutes, then spoon the crusty white layer of salt particles off the top. Underneath is the clear liquid known as clarified butter. The milky liquid at the bottom can be discarded or used in a white sauce. Cover and refrigerate.

Bacon chop with spiced kumquats

Bacon chop is also delicious served just with fried banana or pickled peaches. Buy bacon with a decent layer of fat and the rind still attached for extra flavour and succulence. **Serves 4–5**

900g (2lb) loin of bacon
  (boneless and without the
  streaky end) or streaky
  bacon or thick gammon
  steak
50g (2oz) seasoned rice flour
1 egg, beaten with a little milk
Fresh gluten-free breadcrumbs
  (see page 118)

25g (1oz) clarified butter (see
  page 112) or 15g (½oz)
  butter and 1–2 tablespoons
  extra virgin olive oil, for
  frying
Spiced kumquats (see recipe)

Cover the piece of bacon with cold water. Bring to the boil. If the bacon is salty, discard the water and start again; you may need to do this twice or in extreme cases three times. After the blanching process is completed bring the water to the boil and continue to boil for 45–60 minutes or until fully cooked.

Remove the rind and trim away the excess fat – 1cm (½in) of fat is quite acceptable. Slice the bacon into chops 1–2cm (½–¾in) thick. Dip in seasoned rice flour, then in beaten egg and finally coat with gluten-free breadcrumbs.

Heat the clarified butter or butter and oil in a heavy-based frying pan and fry the chops gently until they are cooked through and golden on both sides.

Serve on hot plates with Spiced Kumquats.

Per serving without kumquats: 523 kcals, 29g fat, 12g saturated fat, 19g carbohydrate, 1.79g sodium, 49mg calcium

Spiced kumquats

Makes 1–2 jars, depending on size

350g (12oz) kumquats
275g (10oz) sugar
225ml (8fl oz) white wine
  vinegar

5cm (2in) piece of cinnamon
  stick
8 whole cloves
2 blades of mace

Rinse the kumquats. Put them into a stainless-steel saucepan. Cover with cold water. Bring to the boil, cover and simmer for about 15 minutes or until the kumquats are tender.

Meanwhile, in another stainless-steel saucepan, dissolve the sugar in the white wine vinegar, add the cinnamon, cloves and mace and stir until it comes to the boil. Drain all the liquid off the kumquats and reserve in case you need it. Put the kumquats into the vinegar syrup and if necessary use some of the reserved cooking liquid to ensure the fruit is covered. Simmer for about 10 minutes until the kumquats look transparent and slightly candied.

Use at once or put the fruit in sterilised glass jars, top up with boiling syrup and immediately cover tightly (not with a tin lid). Label and leave to mature; they keep for several months.

Per recipe: 1336 kcals, 2g fat, 0g saturated fat, 348g carbohydrate, 0.09g sodium, 153mg calcium

Pork en croûte with mushroom and thyme leaf stuffing and bramley apple sauce

This is an impressive dinner-party main course which Rosemary makes with rice paper wrappers. **Serves 6**

2 pork fillets
4 large rice paper wrappers
Egg wash
Bramley Apple Sauce
  (see recipe)
For the marinade
3 tablespoons extra virgin olive
  oil
3 tablespoons lemon juice
3 sprigs of parsley
Sprig of thyme or fennel
1 bay leaf

1 garlic clove, crushed
Salt and freshly ground black
  pepper
**For the mushroom and
thyme leaf stuffing**
15g (½oz) butter
50g (2oz) onions, chopped
225g (8oz) mushrooms, finely
  chopped
2 teaspoons fresh thyme
  leaves

Mix all the ingredients for the marinade in a bowl and marinate the pork for 3–4 hours.

Meanwhile make the stuffing. Sweat the onions in the butter until soft but not coloured. Increase the heat and add the mushrooms, toss until cooked, then add the fresh thyme leaves. Season to taste.

Preheat the oven to 220°C/425°F/gas mark 7.

Trim the pork fillets of all fat. Split the fillets down one side and open out flat. Season with salt and pepper. Divide the stuffing between both pork fillets and fold the meat over.

Dip two rice paper wrappers in hot water for 5–10 seconds. Take care as the softened wrappers are easily torn. Remove and place them, slightly overlapping, on a clean, dry tea-towel. Lay a pork fillet on top. Fold the rice paper wrapper over the meat and turn in the edges to make a neat parcel. Repeat with the remaining wrappers and the second pork fillet. Place on a roasting tray.

Egg-wash the parcels and bake in the oven for 10 minutes, then reduce the temperature to 180°/350°F/gas mark 4 and continue to cook for 30 minutes or until the pork is cooked through but still nice and juicy, and the rice paper wrappers are golden brown.

Serve in slices on hot plates with Bramley Apple Sauce.

Per serving with apple sauce: 266 kcals, 10g fat, 4g saturated fat, 12g carbohydrate, 0.24g sodium, 30mg calcium

Bramley apple sauce
Serves 10

450g (1lb) cooking apples
  (Bramleys, Seedling or
  Grenadier)

50g (2oz) sugar, depending on
  how tart the apples are
2–4 teaspoons water

Peel, quarter and core the apples; cut the pieces in two and put them in a stainless-steel or cast-iron saucepan with the sugar and water. Cover and cook on a very low heat until the apples break down in a fluff. (The trick with apple sauce is to cook it on a very low heat with only a tiny drop of water so it is nice and thick and not too watery.) Stir and taste for sweetness.

Serve warm or cold.

Note: It's always worth having little tubs in the freezer in case you feel like a juicy pork chop or some duck for supper.

Per serving: 35 kcals, 0g fat, 0g saturated fat, 9g carbohydrate, 0g sodium, 2mg calcium

6

Breads and Biscuits

White soda bread

This soda bread is a far cry from the crumbly, dry offerings coeliacs considered to be bread in the past! If you make a loaf especially for breadcrumbs, you could freeze batches for future use. **Makes 1 x 750g (1lb 10oz) loaf**

275g (10oz) rice flour
110g (4oz) tapioca flour
50g (2oz) dried milk
1 scant teaspoon bicarbonate
  of soda
1 heaped teaspoon gluten-free
  baking powder

1 teaspoon salt
1 heaped teaspoon xanthan gum
2 tablespoons caster sugar
1 egg, preferably free range,
  lightly beaten
300–350ml (10–12fl oz)
  buttermilk

Preheat the oven to 230°C/450°F/gas mark 8.

Sift all the dry ingredients together into a large bowl. Mix well by lifting the dry ingredients up into your hands and then letting them fall back into the bowl through your fingers. This adds more air and therefore hopefully more lightness to your finished bread. Lightly whisk the egg and buttermilk together. Make a well in the centre and pour in most of the egg and buttermilk at once. Using one hand, with your fingers stiff and outstretched (like a claw!), stir in a full circular movement from the centre to the outside of the bowl in ever-increasing circles, adding a little more buttermilk if necessary. The dough should be softish, not too wet and sticky.

The trick with white soda bread is not to over-mix the dough. Mix it as quickly and as gently as possible, thus keeping it light and airy. When the dough all comes together, turn it out onto a rice-floured work surface.

Wash and dry your hands. With rice-floured fingers, roll lightly for a few seconds – just enough to tidy it up. Pat the dough into a round, pressing it to about 5cm (2in) in height.

Place the dough on a baking tray dusted lightly with rice flour. With a sharp knife cut a deep cross in it, letting the cuts go over the sides of the bread. Prick with a knife at four angles which, according to Irish folklore, is to let the fairies out!

Bake in the oven for 5 minutes, then reduce the temperature to 180°C/350°F/gas mark 4 for a further 25–30 minutes or until cooked. If in doubt, tap the bottom of the bread: if it is cooked, it will sound hollow. Cool on a wire rack.

Serve freshly baked, cut into thick slices and smeared with butter and homemade jam.

Note: This soda bread is best served the day it is made. However, it tastes lovely toasted the next day. If there is any bread left over, I whiz it in a food processor and keep the gluten-free breadcrumbs in the freezer for future use.

Per loaf: 1611 kcals, 235g fat, 12g saturated fat, 318g carbohydrate, 5.04g sodium, 1118mg calcium

Variations

Spotted dog *This is called railway cake in some parts of Ireland: 'a currant for each station'.*
Follow the master recipe, adding 110g (4oz) sultanas to the dry ingredients. Serve with butter and raspberry jam; it is also delicious eaten with cheese.

White soda bread with herbs
Follow the master recipe, adding 1–2 tablespoons freshly chopped herbs (rosemary, sage, thyme, chives, parsley or lemon balm) to the dry ingredients.

White soda bread with cumin
Follow the master recipe, adding 1–2 tablespoons freshly roasted cumin seeds to the flour.

Seedy bread
If you like caraway seeds, this variation is a must and is delicious served for afternoon tea. Follow the master recipe, adding 1 tablespoon sugar and 2–3 teaspoons caraway seeds to the dry ingredients.

Brown soda bread
A wonderfully nutritious loaf, full of fibre and goodness. It is best eaten on the day it is made, but still tastes good, toasted, with butter and a little homemade jam for a day or two. **Makes 1 x 600g (1lb 4oz) loaf**

50g (2oz) sunflower seeds	1 teaspoon gluten-free baking
110g (4oz) rice flour	powder
60g (2½oz) rice bran	½ teaspoon salt
50g (2oz) tapioca flour	1 teaspoon xanthan gum
25g (1oz) buckwheat flour	1 tablespoon sugar
25g (1oz) dried milk	1 egg, preferably free range
1 scant teaspoon bicarbonate	175–200ml (6–7fl oz)
of soda	buttermilk

Preheat the oven to 230°C/450°F/gas mark 8.

Chop the sunflower seeds very finely or alternatively place in the bowl of a food processor and whiz for 30 seconds.

Place the sunflower seeds in a large mixing bowl and sift in the remainder of the dry ingredients.

Lightly whisk the egg and mix with the buttermilk. Make a well in the centre of the dry ingredients and add almost all of the liquid at once. Using one hand, stir in a full circle, starting in the centre of the bowl and working towards the outside until all the flour is incorporated, adding the remaining or a little extra buttermilk if necessary. The dough should be soft but not too wet and sticky. When it all comes together (a matter of seconds), turn it out onto a rice-floured board.

Wash and dry your hands. Roll the dough around gently for a second, just enough to tidy it up. Flip over and flatten slightly to a depth of about 5cm (2in). Sprinkle a little rice flour onto a baking sheet and place the loaf on top of the rice flour.

Cut a deep cross on the loaf, prick in the four corners, to let the fairies out, and bake in the oven for 5 minutes before reducing the temperature to 180°C/350°F/gas mark 4 for a further 25–30 minutes, or until the bread is cooked. You may wish to turn the loaf upside down in the oven for the final 5 minutes to get the bottom crusty. The loaf will sound hollow when tapped. Leave to cool on a wire rack.

Per loaf: 1543 kcals, 52g fat, 11g saturated fat, 236g carbohydrate, 2.99g sodium, 693mg calcium

White yeast bread
You can make a delicious light brown yeast bread by using 110g (4oz) of rice bran and 150g (5oz) rice flour instead of the 250g (9oz) rice flour in this recipe. **Makes 2 x 900g (2lb) loaves**

250g (9oz) rice flour	40g (1½oz) caster sugar
110g (4oz) fine cornmeal	600ml (1 pint) tepid water
50g (2oz) dried milk	40g (1½oz) fresh yeast
2½ teaspoons xanthan gum	
1 rounded teaspoon salt	2 x 900g (2lb) loaf tins, lined
3 eggs, preferably free range	with parchment paper

Place the rice flour, fine cornmeal, dried milk powder, xanthan gum and salt into a bowl of the food mixer and mix well using the paddle attachment. (Gluten-free flours are very fine and need to be very well blended before any liquid is added. The ingredients should all be at room temperature.)

Whisk the eggs and slowly add to the dry ingredients. Continue to beat for a few minutes on a medium speed.

Dissolve the sugar in 150ml (¼ pint) of the tepid water in a small bowl and crumble in the fresh yeast. Sit the bowl in a warm place to allow the yeast to work. After 4 or 5 minutes it should have a creamy, slightly frothy appearance. Stir and add it gradually, along with the remaining tepid water, into the mixer bowl. Beat well for about 10 minutes. The consistency of the mixture would be too wet to knead by hand.

Spoon the mixture into the lined loaf tins and cover with a clean, slightly damp tea-towel to prevent a skin forming. Leave to rise.

Preheat the oven to 190°C/375°F/gas mark 5.

Just before the bread reaches the top of the tin (about 20 minutes, depending upon the temperature of the kitchen), remove the tea-towel and pop both tins into the fully heated oven. Bake in the oven for 55–60 minutes or until the loaves look nicely browned and sound hollow when tapped. Remove from the tins about 10 minutes before the end of the cooking and put them back into the oven if you like your bread crisp all round. Leave to cool on a wire rack.

Per loaf: 1014 kcals, 18g fat, 7g saturated fat, 192g carbohydrate, 1.83g sodium, 390mg calcium

Sundried tomato cornbread

Here is an appetising variation on cornbread – this one requires no yeast. The mixture can also be baked in muffin tins – great for picnics or lunch boxes. **Makes 1 x 900g (2lb) loaf or 12 muffins**

175g (6oz) fine cornmeal
75g (3oz) rice flour
25g (1oz) soya flour
2 teaspoons gluten-free baking powder
1 teaspoon caster sugar
1 level teaspoon salt
1 teaspoon xanthan gum
50–75g (2–3oz) sun-dried tomatoes (see page 155), chopped

110g (4oz) mature Cheddar cheese, coarsely grated
200ml (7fl oz) tepid milk
2 eggs, preferably free range, beaten
40g (1½oz) butter, melted

900g (2lb) loaf tin, lined with parchment paper or brushed with sunflower oil

Preheat the oven to 180°C/350°F/gas mark 4.

Sift the cornmeal, rice flour, soya flour, gluten-free baking powder, caster sugar, salt and xanthan gum into a large mixing bowl and mix thoroughly. Add the sundried tomatoes and cheese and mix well.

Combine the milk, beaten eggs and melted butter in a measuring jug. Gradually add to the dry ingredients and beat together.

Spoon the mixture into the prepared tin. Bake in the oven for about 50 minutes for the loaf, 25 minutes for muffins, or until the bread has risen and is golden brown. Remove from the tin and bake for a further 5–10 minutes until it sounds hollow when tapped. Leave to cool on a wire rack.

Per loaf: 2119 kcals, 100g fat, 55g saturated fat, 230g carbohydrate, 5.08g sodium, 1440mg calcium

Cornmeal bread

This is the basic recipe for cornbread which you can vary to your taste. A little chopped chilli pepper and rosemary are good. Alternatively, just add some chilli powder or flakes. **Makes 1 x 900g (2lb) loaf**

200g (7oz) fine cornmeal
160g (5½oz) rice flour
2½ rounded teaspoons
    xanthan gum
50g (2oz) dried milk
1½ teaspoons salt
50g (2oz) caster sugar
300ml (10fl oz) tepid water

1 tablespoon dried active yeast
1 teaspoon white wine vinegar
3 medium eggs, preferably free
    range, beaten

900g (2lb) loaf tin, lined with
    parchment paper or brushed
    with sunflower oil

Sift the fine cornmeal, rice flour and xanthan gum into the bowl of a food mixer. Add the dried milk and salt and then mix well.

Dissolve the sugar in the measured tepid water in a small bowl and sprinkle in the dried yeast. Sit the bowl in a warm place to allow the yeast to work. After 4 or 5 minutes it should have a creamy, slightly frothy appearance.

Meanwhile mix the white wine vinegar with the beaten eggs and pour into the bowl of the food mixer. Mix well through the dry ingredients using the paddle of the mixer.

When the yeast mixture is ready, stir it, then pour into the bowl of the mixer. The mixture should be too wet to knead and be slightly lumpy. Mix on a medium speed for about 10 minutes (using the K-blade) until a smooth, free-flowing, thick batter-like consistency is achieved.

Pour the contents of the bowl into the prepared loaf tin. Cover with a single sheet of clingfilm, which has been lightly brushed with a tasteless oil, such as sunflower oil, to prevent a skin from forming.

Preheat the oven to 190°C/375°F/gas mark 5.

Just before the bread reaches the top of the tin (which takes between 20 and 40 minutes, depending on the temperature of the kitchen), remove the clingfilm. Place the loaf in the oven and bake for approximately 45 minutes. Remove the loaf from the tin and return to the oven for a further 10 minutes or until the bread is golden brown and sounds hollow when tapped. Leave to cool on a wire rack.

Per loaf: 1945 kcals, 37g fat, 14g saturated fat, 357g carbohydrate, 3.44g sodium, 690mg calcium

Naan bread

Naan is an Indian flat bread traditionally baked in a tandoor oven. We've cooked great naan in the oven, then browned them under a hot grill. Add 2 tablespoons of chopped spring onions to the dry ingredients for variety. **Makes 6**

150ml (¼ pint) tepid milk
2 teaspoons caster sugar
2 teaspoons dried active yeast
275g (10oz) rice flour
175g (6oz) tapioca flour
1 teaspoon xanthan gum
½ teaspoon salt
1 teaspoon gluten-free baking powder
2 tablespoons vegetable oil
150ml (5fl oz) natural yogurt, lightly beaten
1 egg, preferably free range, lightly beaten

Pour the tepid milk into a small bowl, add 1 teaspoon of the sugar and sprinkle in the dried yeast. Sit the bowl in a warm place to allow the yeast to work. After 4 or 5 minutes it should have a creamy, slightly frothy appearance.

Sift the rice flour, tapioca flour, xanthan gum, salt and gluten-free baking powder into the bowl of a food mixer. Add the remaining sugar, the oil, yogurt and lightly beaten egg. Using the paddle attachment, mix the contents together for 8–10 minutes until a smooth and satiny ball of dough is formed.

Preheat the oven to its highest setting. Put your heaviest baking tray to heat in the oven and preheat the grill.

When the dough is ready, remove it from the food mixer and divide it into 6 equal-sized balls. Keep 5 of them covered with a clean tea-towel while you work with the first. Roll this ball into a tear-shaped naan, about 25cm (10in) in length and about 12cm (5in) at its widest, using a little rice flour if necessary. Roll out a second naan in this way.

Remove the hot tray from the oven and slap the two naans onto it. Put it immediately into the oven for 3 minutes. The naan should puff up. Place the tray and naan under a hot grill, about 7–10cm (3–4in) from the heat, for about 30 seconds or until the top of the naan browns slightly. Wrap in a clean tea-towel to keep them hot and soft while you cook the rest in the same way.

Per serving: 357 kcals, 6g fat, 1g saturated fat, 73g carbohydrate, 0.32g sodium, 108mg calcium

Fruit scones

The yogurt helps to produce a light and tender scone. Use plump yellow sultanas or lexia raisins for extra a treat or substitute chopped chocolate and/or nuts for the sultanas. Or try dried cherries or chopped Medjool dates. **Makes 15**

275g (10oz) rice flour
50g (2oz) tapioca flour
4 teaspoons gluten-free baking powder
2 teaspoons xanthan gum
1 teaspoon salt
4 tablespoons caster sugar
110g (4oz) butter
110g (4oz) sultanas
2 eggs, preferably free range
125ml–175ml (4–6fl oz) natural yogurt
Egg wash

Preheat the oven to 250°C/475°F/gas mark 9.

Sift all the dry ingredients into a large bowl and mix well. Rub in the butter. Add the sultanas and gently mix together.

Lightly whisk the eggs and natural yogurt together.

Make a well in the centre of the dry ingredients and add the egg and yogurt mixture. Mix to a soft dough, adding a little more natural yogurt if necessary.

Turn onto a rice-floured board and knead lightly, just enough to shape into a round. Roll out to about 2.5cm (1in) thick and stamp into scones using a 5.5cm (2¼in) cutter. Place on a rice-floured baking sheet and brush with a little egg wash.

Bake for approximately 10 minutes until golden brown on top. Leave to cool on a wire rack.

Serve split in half with butter and homemade raspberry jam.

Per scone: 204 kcals, 8g fat, 5g saturated fat, 31g carbohydrate, 0.38g sodium, 50mg calcium

Lemon shortbread biscuits

One can never have too many biscuit recipes – and these biscuits have good keeping qualities if stored in an airtight tin. They are perfect for picnics. **Makes about 35**

175g (6oz) butter
75g (3oz) caster sugar, plus extra for sprinkling
Grated rind of 3 lemons
175g (6oz) rice flour, plus extra for dusting
75g (3oz) ground almonds

Preheat the oven to 180°C/350°F/gas mark 4.

Cream the butter until soft. Add the sugar and lemon rind and beat until light and fluffy. Add the rice flour and ground almonds and mix until combined.

Knead lightly until the dough is smooth. Cover and refrigerate for about 1 hour, which will make the dough firmer and easier to handle.

Roll out the dough on a rice-floured work surface to a thickness of 5mm (¼in). Alternatively, roll out the pastry between two sheets of parchment paper. Stamp into rounds with a 4 cm(1½in) cutter. Place on several baking sheets and bake, in batches if necessary, for 10–15 minutes until golden.

Leave the biscuits to cool for a few minutes on the baking sheet before transferring to a cooling rack.

Sprinkle with caster sugar before serving.

Per biscuit: 80 kcals, 5g fat, 3g saturated fat, 8g carbohydrate, 0.04g sodium, 8mg calcium

Coconut and raspberry biscuits

These rich little slices take a bit of time to make but the end result is worth every second. This does mean, though, that they will seem to disappear at the speed of light! **Makes 24**

For the base
140g (4½oz) butter, softened
60g (2½oz) caster sugar
1 egg, preferably free range, beaten
1 teaspoon pure vanilla extract
100g (3½oz) rice flour
75g (3oz) tapioca flour
1 teaspoon gluten–free baking powder
1 teaspoon xanthan gum
50ml (2fl oz) milk

For the filling
175g (6oz) raspberry jam
250g (9oz) raspberries
For the topping
100g (3½oz) butter, softened
150g (5oz) caster sugar
2 eggs, preferably free range, lightly beaten
225g (8oz) desiccated coconut
60g (2½oz) rice flour
Swiss roll tin, 20 x 30cm (8 x 12in), lined with parchment paper

Preheat the oven to 180°C/350°F/gas mark 4.

To make the base, cream the butter and gradually add the caster sugar. Beat until pale, soft and light. Add the egg, a little at a time, beating well after each addition, before adding the vanilla extract.

Sift together the dry ingredients and stir gently into the creamed mixture. Mix everything together lightly and add the milk to moisten. Spread the mixture into the prepared tin, smoothing it out to the edges. Spread the jam gently over the cake mixture and sprinkle with the raspberries. You may need to press them down gently into the cake mixture.

Make the topping. Cream the butter and sugar together as before until pale, soft and light. Add the beaten eggs gradually, beating well after each addition. Mix together the coconut and rice flour and fold into the mixture. Spread gently but evenly over the raspberries and bake in the oven for about 35–40 minutes or until a skewer comes out cleanly.

Leave to cool in the tin and cut into 24 biscuits.

Per biscuit: 240 kcals, 16g fat, 11g saturated fat, 24g carbohydrate, 0.12g sodium, 20mg calcium

Brownies

One of the simplest, tastiest and most popular of recipes – it is the relatively high sugar content that gives brownies their delicious and characteristic crust. Do buy a chocolate with at least 70 per cent cocoa solids for real flavour. **Makes 16**

50g (2oz) best-quality
   gluten-free dark chocolate
100g (3½oz) butter
200g (7oz) caster sugar
2 eggs, preferably free range,
   lightly whisked
½ teaspoon pure vanilla
   extract

75g (3oz) ground almonds
½ teaspoon gluten-free baking
   powder
Pinch of salt
110g (4oz) chopped walnuts

20cm (8in) square tin, lined
   with silicone paper

Preheat the oven to 180°C/350°F/gas mark 4.

Melt the chocolate in a heatproof bowl suspended over a pan of simmering water or in a low oven.

Cream the butter and sugar until pale, soft and light, then beat in the lightly whisked eggs, the vanilla extract and melted chocolate. Lastly stir in the ground almonds, gluten-free baking powder, salt and chopped nuts. Spread the mixture in the tin and bake in the oven for about 30–35 minutes.

Leave to cool, then cut into 5cm (2in) squares for serving.

Per brownie: 207 kcals, 15g fat, 5g saturated fat, 15g carbohydrate, 0.13g sodium, 28mg calcium

Chocolate orange hazelnut biscuits

This recipe can also be served as a tart using Rosemary's sweet pastry (page 136) and a 23cm (9in) tart tin. Serve with crème fraîche (see page 64). **Makes 12**

For the base
75g (3oz) tapioca flour
75g (3oz) rice flour
25g (1oz) caster sugar
110g (4oz) butter
Drop of pure vanilla extract
1 egg yolk, preferably free
    range

For the topping
200g (7oz) hazelnuts
75g (3oz) best-quality
    gluten-free dark chocolate
    (70% cocoa solids)

75g (3oz) butter, preferably
    unsalted
150g (5oz) caster sugar
2 eggs, preferably free range,
    beaten
1 teaspoon freshly grated
    orange rind
25g (1oz) rice flour
3 tablespoons freshly squeezed
    orange juice

20 x 30cm (8 x 10in) tin,
    greased

Preheat the oven to 180°C/350°F/gas mark 4.

Combine the dry ingredients for the base, rub in the butter, then add the vanilla extract and bind with the egg yolk. Press into the prepared tin, prick with a fork and bake in the oven for 10–15 minutes or until golden.

Meanwhile, put the hazelnuts on a baking sheet and roast in the oven for 5–7 minutes or until the skins loosen. Put the hazelnuts in a clean tea-towel and rub off the skins. Chop them roughly.

Chop the chocolate into small pieces. Cream the butter with the sugar until pale, soft and light. Add one egg. Lightly beat in the remaining ingredients, adding the second egg last. Spread the mixture onto the cooked pastry base and bake for 20–25 minutes. Leave to cool, then cut into 12 squares.

Per biscuit: 397 kcals, 28g fat, 11g saturated fat, 32g carbohydrate, 0.1g sodium, 41mg calcium

Anzac biscuits
These crunchy biscuits commemorate the participation of Australia and New Zealand in the Second World War. Here is the coeliac-friendly version: they're so good you may need to hide them! **Makes 30**

110g (4oz) millet flakes
110g (4oz) caster sugar
110g (4oz) desiccated
    coconut
50g (2oz) rice flour
50g (2oz) tapioca flour

50g (2oz) ground almonds
3 tablespoons water
1 tablespoon golden syrup
110g (4oz) butter
2 teaspoons bicarbonate
    of soda

Preheat the oven to 160°C/325°F/gas mark 3.

Mix together all the dry ingredients except the bicarbonate of soda in a bowl.

Put the water, golden syrup and butter into a small saucepan, bring to the boil, then remove from the heat, add the bicarbonate of soda and stir. Pour into the dry ingredients and mix thoroughly.

Roll the mixture into balls and place onto a baking sheet lined with parchment paper. Space them sufficiently far apart for the biscuits to spread as they cook. Flatten with a fork and bake in the oven for 20 minutes or until golden brown.

Leave to cool on the baking sheet for about 5–6 minutes, or until firm enough to handle, before transferring to a wire rack to cool completely.

Store in an airtight container.

Per biscuit: 110 kcals, 7g fat, 4g saturated fat, 11g carbohydrate, 0.15g sodium, 7mg calcium

Frosted lemon squares

These fresh-tasting treats are delicious with a cup of tea or coffee but also make a scrummy pud served with fresh berries and a blob of crème fraîche (see page 64). **Makes 18**

175g (6oz) butter, softened
175g (6oz) caster sugar
2 eggs, preferably free range
75g (3oz) rice flour
75g (3oz) tapioca flour
1½ teaspoons gluten-free
   baking powder
1 teaspoon xanthan gum

For the frosting
Freshly grated rind and juice of
   1 lemon
110g (4oz) caster sugar

Swiss roll tin, 25 x 18cm
   (10 x 7in), well greased

Preheat the oven to 180°C/350°F/gas mark 4.

Put the butter, sugar, eggs, rice flour, tapioca flour, gluten-free baking powder and xanthan gum into the bowl of a food processor. Whiz together for a few seconds to amalgamate. Spread the mixture evenly in the prepared tin and bake for 25–35 minutes or until pale golden brown.

Meanwhile mix all the ingredients for the frosting in a bowl. As soon as the biscuits are cooked, spoon a little of the frosting over the top at a time, allowing it to soak through before pouring on more. Leave to cool in the tin. Cut into squares.

Per biscuit: 177 kcals, 9g fat, 5g saturated fat, 25g carbohydrate, 0.13g sodium, 15mg calcium

Caramelised almond squares

These will quickly become another of your favourite biscuits. They are quite rich, so cut them into tiny squares to serve with coffee after dinner. **Makes 24**

110g (4oz) tapioca flour
75g (3oz) rice flour
25g (1oz) caster sugar
110g (4oz) butter
Drop of pure vanilla extract
1 egg yolk, preferably free
   range

For the topping
175g (6oz) flaked almonds
75g (3oz) butter
3 tablespoons set honey
40g (1¼oz) soft brown sugar
1 tablespoon single cream

Swiss roll tin, 20 x 30cm
   (8 x 12 in), well greased

Preheat the oven to 180°C/350°F/gas mark 4.

Put the tapioca flour, rice flour and sugar into a bowl, rub in the butter, add the vanilla extract and bind with the egg yolk. Press into the prepared tin, prick with a fork and bake for 10–15 minutes, or until golden. Remove from the oven and allow the pastry base to cool for a few minutes.

Put all the ingredients for the topping except the cream, into a saucepan and cook over a low heat until the mixture is a pale straw colour. Stir in the cream and cook for a few more seconds. Spread the mixture over the cooked base and return it to the oven until the topping is a deep golden colour – anything from 8 to 20 minutes, depending on the length of time the original ingredients were cooked.

Leave the biscuits to cool in the tin for 10 minutes before cutting into 5cm (2in) squares. Remove from the tin and cool fully on a wire rack.

Per biscuit: 157 kcals, 11g fat, 5g saturated fat, 12g carbohydrate, 0.07g sodium, 23mg calcium

Almond fingers

You can use these fingers as the basis of tiramisu or simply enjoy them to nibble with a cup of tea or coffee. Make sure the ground almonds haven't been bulked out with flour. **Makes 30–32**

6 eggs, preferably-free range
175g (6oz) caster sugar
50g (2oz) butter, melted
110g (4oz) ground almonds

25g (1oz) rice flour
2 x Swiss roll tins, 20 x 30cm (8 x 12in), lined with parchment or silicone paper

Preheat the oven to 180°C/ 350°F/gas mark 4.

Beat the eggs and sugar together using an electric whisk until they are pale, thick and mousse-like. Gently stir in the cooled melted butter. Mix the ground almonds with the rice flour and fold through the egg mixture.

Pour the mixture into the prepared Swiss roll tins and bake in the oven for 15 minutes or until golden in colour and firm to the touch.

Leave to cool, then cut 16 almond fingers out of each tray.

Per biscuit: 81 kcals, 5g fat, 1g saturated fat, 7g carbohydrate, 0.03g sodium, 18mg calcium

Crispy cheese biscuits

A tasty way to use up leftover cheese – it can be a mixture, but don't have too high a proportion of blue cheese or the biscuits will be too strongly flavoured. **Makes 12**

50g (2oz) butter, softened
50g (2oz) potato flour, plus extra for dusting

1 teaspoon xanthan gum
50g (2oz) mature Cheddar cheese, grated

Preheat the oven to 230°C/450°F/gas mark 8.

Cream the butter until pale and soft. Add the potato flour and xanthan gum. Mix together and add the grated cheese, and continue to mix until all the dry ingredients are incorporated into the soft butter. Alternatively, just place all the ingredients into the bowl of a food processor and whiz until a smooth dough is formed.

Sprinkle a little potato flour on the work surface and roll the dough into a sausage shape, approximately 4cm (1½in) wide. Wrap in clingfilm and refrigerate until firm – for about 1½ hours.

Cut the dough into equal slices about 8mm (⅓in) thick and place directly onto a baking sheet. Bake in the oven for 6 minutes or until pale golden.

Leave to cool on the baking sheet for 2 minutes before transferring to a cooling rack using a palette knife. Store in an airtight container.

Per biscuit: 63 kcals, 5g fat, 3g saturated fat, 3g carbohydrate, 0.06g sodium, 33mg calcium

7 Cakes and Puddings

Ballymaloe chocolate almond gâteau

It's worth choosing the best chocolate you can: look for Valrhona, Menier, Suchard, Lesmé or Callebaut. If you can stop yourself from finishing this in one sitting, this cake keeps well. **Serves 8–10**

110g (4oz) best-quality
gluten-free dark chocolate
(70% cocoa solids)

2 tablespoons red Jamaica rum

110g (4oz) whole almonds

110g (4oz) butter, preferably
unsalted

110g (4oz) caster sugar, plus
1 tablespoon extra, to mix
with the egg whites

3 eggs, preferably free range,
separated

For the chocolate icing

110g (4oz) best-quality
gluten-free dark chocolate
(70% cocoa solids)

2 tablespoons red Jamaica rum

110g (4oz) unsalted butter

To decorate

Crystallised violets

Flaked almonds

2 x 18cm (7in) sandwich tins

Preheat the oven to 180°C/350°F/gas mark 4.

Line the base of each of the tins with a round of greaseproof paper. Brush the bottom and sides with melted butter and dust with a little rice flour.

Melt the chocolate with the rum in a heatproof bowl over a pan of simmering water or in a low oven.

Bring a small saucepan of water to the boil and add the almonds. Bring back to the boil for 2–3 minutes and then test an almond to see if the skin is loose. Drain the almonds, peel and discard the skins. Grind the whole almonds in a food processor until they are slightly gritty.

Cream the butter, and add the sugar. Beat until pale, light and soft. Beat in the egg yolks, one by one. Whisk the egg whites until stiff. Add the extra tablespoon of sugar and continue to whisk until stiff peaks form, then add the melted chocolate to the butter and sugar mixture. Divide the prepared almonds roughly into four portions. Add one portion to the creamed mixture. Fold in a quarter of the egg white, followed by more almonds. Fold in the remaining eggs and almonds alternately until they have all been added.

Divide the mixture between the two prepared tins and make a hollow in the centre of each cake. Bake in the oven for about 20–25 minutes. The sides should be cooked but the centre still a little unset. Leave to cool for a few minutes in the tins, turn out gently onto a wire rack, remove the paper and allow to become completely cold.

To make the icing, melt the chocolate with the rum in a heatproof bowl over a pan of simmering water or in a low oven. Whisk in the butter, a tablespoon at a time, until melted. Remove from the heat and whisk occasionally until cool. If the icing seems too runny, put the bowl in the fridge and allow to firm up, whisk to lighten and then use.

When the cake is completely cold, fill and ice with the chocolate mixture. (If you want to cover the sides and pipe the a border around the top, make 1½ times the quantity of icing.) Decorate with flaked almonds and crystallised violets.

Per serving: 640 kcals, 51g fat, 24g saturated fat, 36g carbohydrate, 0.15g sodium, 73mg calcium

Californian lemon polenta cake

This delicious moist and fresh-tasting cake keeps really well. It is great served as a teatime cake or as a pudding accompanied by a few fresh summer berries and sour cream. **Serves 8–10**

225g (8oz) butter, softened
225g (8oz) caster sugar
225g (8oz) ground almonds
1 teaspoon pure vanilla extract
3 eggs, preferably free range, lightly beaten
Grated rind of 2 unwaxed and washed lemons and the juice of 1 lemon
110g (4oz) fine cornmeal (polenta)
1 teaspoon gluten-free baking powder
Pinch of salt

To serve

Summer fruit in season (raspberries, strawberries, blueberries, etc)
Sour cream

23cm (9in) spring-form cake tin

Preheat the oven to 160°C/325°F/gas mark 3.

Brush the cake tin with a little melted butter and flour the tin with rice flour. Cut out a round of parchment paper for the base of the tin.

In a large mixing bowl beat the butter until pale and soft. Add the sugar and beat again until light and creamy. Stir in the ground almonds and vanilla extract. Add the eggs, a little at a time, and beat thoroughly between additions. Fold in the lemon rind and juice, cornmeal, gluten-free baking powder and salt.

Pour the mixture into the prepared tin and bake for about 50 minutes or until the top of the cake is deep golden and a skewer inserted into the centre comes out clean. Cool on a wire rack and remove the paper.

Serve in slices with some summer berries and a blob of sour cream.

Per serving: 634 kcals, 46g fat, 18g saturated fat, 47g carbohydrate, 0.44g sodium, 105mg calcium

Banana bread

Soft, speckled bananas are best for this recipe. The mixture also makes adorable little mini muffins if you cook them in individual cases – great for children's packed lunches. Big kids like them too! **Makes 1 x 900g (2lb) loaf**

40g (1½oz) cherries
75g (3oz) sultanas
110g (4oz) butter, softened
110g (4oz) caster sugar
2 large eggs, preferably free range
3 large ripe bananas
175g (6oz) fine rice flour
50g (2oz) cornflour
2 teaspoons gluten-free baking powder
½ teaspoon salt

1kg (2lb) loaf tin, lined with parchment paper, or
24 small paper muffin cases

Preheat the oven to 180°C/350°F/gas mark 4.

Wash and dry the cherries. Cut into quarters and mix with the sultanas. Set aside.

Cream the butter and sugar together until pale, light and soft. Add the eggs, one by one, and beat well between each addition.

Mash the bananas and add to the creamed mixture. Sift the rice flour, cornflour, gluten-free baking powder and salt together and fold carefully into the banana mixture. Very gently, stir in the cherries and sultanas, so that they are evenly distributed through the mixture.

Pour the mixture into the loaf tin or into 24 small muffin cases and bake in the oven for about 1¼–1½ hours for the loaf, 25 minutes for the mini muffins, until golden on top and a skewer inserted into the centre comes out clean.

Remove the loaf from the tin and cool on a wire rack; cool mini muffins on a rack in their paper cases. Slice the loaf into 8 slices to serve.

Per serving: 388 kcals, 15g fat, 9g saturated fat, 63g carbohydrate, 0.42g sodium, 45mg calcium

Chocolate and raspberry torte

We think this is the ultimate chocolate torte. It's certainly no sacrifice to tuck into this cake – sheer indulgence. Keep your portions small: a little goes a long way! **Serves 8–10**

200g (7oz) best-quality gluten-free dark chocolate (70% cocoa solids)
50g (2oz) butter
3 eggs, preferably free range, separated

50g (2oz) caster sugar
50ml (2fl oz) single cream
110g (4oz) ground almonds
150g (5oz) raspberries

20cm (8in) spring-form tin

Preheat the oven to 180°C/350°F/gas mark 4.

Line the base of the tin with parchment paper and brush the sides with a little melted butter, followed by a dusting of ground almonds.

Place the chocolate and the butter in a heatproof bowl over a pan of simmering water or in a low oven. Use an electric whisk to beat the egg yolks with the sugar until pale, light and soft. When the chocolate and butter mixture has melted, add to the creamed mixture and mix well to combine. Stir in the single cream and the ground almonds.

In a large, scrupulously clean bowl beat the egg whites until stiff peaks form. Very gently fold the egg whites, a third at a time, into the chocolate mixture. Next, gently fold in the raspberries. Pour into the prepared spring-form tin.

Bake in the oven for about 25–30 minutes. The sides should be cooked but the centre should be slightly underdone.

Leave the cake to cool completely in the tin before turning out. Serve a little slice with softly whipped cream and a few extra fresh raspberries.

Per serving: 358 kcals, 28g fat, 11g saturated fat, 20g carbohydrate, 0.08g sodium, 72mg calcium

Fresh strawberry sponge

Oozing with fresh summer fruit and softly whipped cream… this is irresistible. The cake keeps brilliantly in an airtight tin. Serve cream separately if you don't plan to eat it all in one go! **Serves 8**

140g (4½oz) butter
175g (6oz) caster sugar
3 eggs, preferably free range
110g (4oz) rice flour
50g (2oz) ground almonds
1½ teaspoons gluten-free baking powder
1 teaspoon xanthan gum
1 tablespoon milk

For the filling
300ml (10fl oz) whipping cream, softly whipped
225g (8oz) fresh strawberries, sliced
Caster sugar, for dusting

2 x 18cm (7in) sandwich tins

Preheat the oven to 180°C/350°F/gas mark 4.

Grease the two cake tins and dust with rice flour, then line the base of each with a round of greaseproof paper.

Cream the butter, gradually add the sugar and beat until pale, light and soft. Add the eggs, one at a time, and beat well between each addition. (If the butter and the sugar are not creamed properly and if you add the eggs too fast, the mixture will curdle, resulting in a cake with a heavier texture.)

Sift the rice flour, ground almonds, baking powder and xanthan gum together and stir in gradually. Mix all together lightly and add the milk to moisten.

Divide the mixture evenly between the tins and make a slight hollow in the centre. Bake for about 20–25 minutes or until a skewer inserted into the centre comes out clean. Turn the cakes onto a wire rack and leave to cool.

Sandwich the cakes together with the whipped cream and sliced strawberries. Dust with sifted caster sugar. Serve on an old-fashioned plate with a doyley.

For a change, homemade raspberry jam, chocolate spread and cream or even bananas and cream are also delicious.

Per serving: 440 kcals, 29g fat, 16g saturated fat, 41g carbohydrate, 0.29g sodium, 70mg calcium

Rosemary's sweet pastry

Gluten-free flours are a little harder to work with, but well worth mastering. Keep the dough dry; although slightly more difficult to handle, it gives a crisper, 'shorter' crust for your tarts and pies. **Makes 425g (15oz)**

75g (3oz) rice flour
75g (3oz) fine cornmeal (polenta)
75g (3oz) potato flour
1 heaped teaspoon xanthan gum

Pinch of salt
150g (5oz) butter
50g (2oz) caster sugar
1 egg, preferably free range, mixed with 2 tablespoons cold water

Sift the rice flour, fine cornmeal, potato flour, xanthan gum and salt into a bowl and mix well. Cut the butter into cubes and gently rub into the flour mixture. Stir in the sugar. Make a well in the centre and carefully add some of the egg and water mixture – just enough to bring the pastry together using a fork. Collect the pastry into a ball with your hands. This way you can judge more accurately whether you need a few more drops of liquid. It is tempting to add extra liquid at this stage but try not to, as it is very easy to make the pastry too wet. It is fine to have some liquid left over. Although rather damp pastry is easier to handle and roll out, the resulting crust can be tough and may well shrink out of shape in the oven.

On a very lightly rice-floured board, gently knead the dough with the heel of your hand for a few minutes to form a silky-smooth ball. Flatten slightly, wrap in clingfilm and refrigerate for about 30 minutes. This will make the pastry much less elastic and easier to roll.

When it has chilled enough, roll it out (between 2 sheets of parchment paper, if necessary, to stop it sticking) and use as required.

Per recipe: 2161 kcals, 132g fat, 80g saturated fat, 232g carbohydrate, 2.04g sodium, 116mg calcium

Rustic summer berry tart

This rustic tart with its filling of gooey summer fruit is one of our favourites. No need to be sorry about the ragged edges: it's meant to be like that.

Serves 6–8

1 quantity Rosemary's sweet pastry (see recipe, left)
Egg wash
Caster sugar, for dusting
For the filling
75g (3oz) caster sugar
2 tablespoons cornflour
110g (4oz) blueberries

110g (4oz) raspberries
2 peaches or nectarines, peeled, stoned and sliced

Deep tart tin, 18cm (7in) diameter, with removable base

Preheat the oven to 180°C/350°F/gas mark 4.

Make the gluten-free pastry following the recipe. Flatten into a round, cover with greaseproof paper and leave to chill. On a very lightly rice-floured work surface, roll out the pastry and line the tart tin, but leave any excess pastry hanging over the edge. Refrigerate.

Make the filling by mixing the sugar with the cornflour in a large bowl. Toss in the blueberries and sliced peaches or nectarines, then add the raspberries, being careful not to crush them. Leave to sit for 5 minutes, tossing occasionally.

Pour the fruit and the juices into the chilled tart shell and distribute evenly. When the dough is pliable, fold in the overhanging edge to cover the outer portion of the filling, leaving an opening of about 7cm (3in) diameter, exposing the fruit in the centre of the pie.

Brush the pastry with a little egg wash and bake in the oven for about 50 minutes or until the pastry is golden brown and cooked through. Sprinkle with a little caster sugar and allow to cool for 10 minutes, which will allow the fruit juices to settle, before removing from the tin.

This tart is delicious served warm or cold together with softly whipped cream.

Per serving: 469 kcals, 23g fat, 14g saturated fat, 63g carbohydrate, 0.36g sodium, 37mg calcium

Besançon apple tart

This is a version of a tart from Besançon in eastern France. Pears, gooseberries, apricots, plums and rhubarb are also good and the custard could be flavoured with a little cinnamon instead of vanilla for a change. **Serves 10–12**

1 quantity Rosemary's sweet pastry (see page 136)
Egg wash
4–6 tablespoons apricot glaze (see recipe)

For the filling
2 or 3 Golden Delicious apples
2 large or 3 small eggs, preferably free range
2 tablespoons caster sugar
1 teaspoon pure vanilla extract
300ml (½ pint) single cream

Tart tin, 30cm (12in) or 2 x 18cm (7in) tart tins with removable base

Preheat the oven to 180°C/350°F/gas mark 4.

Make the gluten-free pastry following the recipe and refrigerate for 1 hour if possible. Line the tin (or tins) with the pastry and chill for 10 minutes. Line with parchment paper and dried beans and bake blind for 15–20 minutes. Remove the paper and beans, brush the tart with a little egg wash and return to the oven for 3–4 minutes. Leave to cool, then brush the base with apricot glaze.

Peel the apples, quarter, core and cut into even slices about 3mm (⅛in) thick. Arrange the slices as you go to form a circle inside the tart, with the slices slightly overlapping on the inside. Fill the centre likewise.

Whisk the eggs well with the sugar and the vanilla extract. Add the cream and strain this mixture over the apples.

Bake in the oven for about 35 minutes. When the custard is set and the apples are fully cooked, brush generously with apricot glaze (this is essential for flavour, not just for appearance).

Serve warm with a bowl of whipped cream.

Per serving, including apricot glaze: 332 kcals, 20g fat, 12g saturated fat, 35g carbohydrate, 0.24g sodium, 48mg calcium

Apricot glaze
Makes about 300ml (½ pint)

375g (13oz) apricot jam

Juice of ½ lemon or 2 tablespoons water

Melt the apricot jam in a small stainless-steel saucepan with 1–2 tablespoons lemon juice or water. Push the hot jam through a nylon sieve and store in a sterilised airtight jar.

Warm and stir the glaze before use if necessary.

Lady Dundee's orange cake

Despite the name association, there is no marmalade in this cake. It is delightfully moist and entirely suitable for coeliacs if gluten-free baking powder is used. **Serves 8**

2 medium oranges, preferably
  organic
3 eggs, preferably free range
250g (9oz) caster sugar
1 teaspoon gluten-free baking
  powder
265g (9½oz) best-quality
  ground almonds

For the topping (optional)
50g (2oz) caster sugar
250g (9oz) mascarpone
Grated rind and juice of
  2 limes
Gluten-free icing sugar
  (optional)

20cm (8in) spring-form tin

Scrub the oranges, put them whole in a saucepan with enough water to cover, and put a lid on the pan. Simmer for 1–2 hours or until the oranges are completely tender. To ensure the skins are not bitter, change the simmering water up to three times.

Preheat the oven to 180°C/350°F/gas mark 4.

Brush the cake tin with a little melted butter and dust with ground almonds. Cut out a round of parchment paper for the base of the tin.

Halve the oranges, remove the pips and purée the flesh and peel in a blender. Beat the eggs and sugar until pale, light and soft. Combine the baking powder and ground almonds, then fold gently into the eggs. Fold in the orange purée.

Pour the mixture into the prepared tin and bake on the centre shelf of the oven for about 1 hour or until a skewer inserted into the centre comes out clean.

Cool on a wire rack and remove the paper.

To make the topping, mix the sugar with the mascarpone, lime rind and juice and spread over the cake. Alternatively, dredge the cake with gluten-free icing sugar.

Per serving, including topping: 492 kcals, 39g fat, 13g saturated fat, 25g carbohydrate, 0.15g sodium, 161mg calcium

Plum tart

Perfect for those who feel that making pastry is not their forte. We vary the filling with the season and the amount of sugar in the filling depends upon the sweetness of the fruit. We leave the stones in the plums, but you don't have to. **Serves 8–12**

225g (8oz) butter
50g (2oz) caster sugar
2 eggs, preferably free range
110g (4oz) rice flour
110g (4oz) fine cornmeal
  (polenta)
110g (4oz) potato flour
2 teaspoons xanthan gum
Egg wash

For the filling
700g (1½lb) plums
110g (4oz) caster sugar
To serve
Caster sugar, for dusting
Softly whipped cream
Barbados sugar

Rectangular tin, 18 x 30 x
  2.5cm (7 x 12 x 1in); 23cm
  (9in) square tin or round tin
  25cm (10in) diameter

First make the pastry. Cream the butter and sugar together by hand or in a food mixer. Add the eggs and beat for several minutes. Reduce the speed and mix in the rice flour, fine cornmeal, potato flour and xanthan gum. Turn the pastry out onto a piece of rice-floured greaseproof paper, flatten into a round, wrap and chill – overnight if possible.

Preheat the oven to 180°C/350°F/gas mark 4.

Roll out the pastry to a thickness of about 3mm (⅛in) and use about two-thirds of it to line a suitable tin. If you find the dough a little difficult to work with, roll it between 2 sheets of parchment paper.

Halve the plums, place them in the pastry-lined tin and sprinkle with sugar. Cover with a lid of pastry, seal the edges and use leftover pastry to decorate the top. Brush with egg wash and bake for 45–60 minutes until the plums are tender. Allow to cool in the tin for about 10 minutes before removing otherwise the sides of the tart will collapse.

Cut into squares, sprinkle lightly with caster sugar and serve with softly whipped cream and Barbados sugar.

Per serving: 529 kcals, 28g fat, 17g saturated fat, 67g carbohydrate, 0.27g sodium, 37mg calcium

Baked raspberry and passion-fruit cheesecake

This cheesecake is truly luscious and decadent: anyone I've made it for requests it time and time again – coeliacs and non-coeliacs alike! Best made a day in advance. **Serves 8–10**

110g (4oz) gluten-free biscuits – Lemon Shortbread Biscuits (page 124) are especially good for this base

110g (4oz) best-quality ground almonds

110g (4oz) butter, melted

For the filling

225g (8oz) mascarpone

225g (8oz) ricotta cheese

125ml (4fl oz) crème fraîche (see page 64)

3 eggs, preferably free range

200g (7oz) caster sugar

1 heaped tablespoon cornflour, slaked with 2 tablespoons water

1 tablespoon finely grated lemon rind

3 tablespoons freshly squeezed lemon juice

3–5 passion-fruit

225g (8oz) raspberries

23cm (9in) spring-form cake tin

Preheat the oven to 150°C/300°F/gas mark 2.

Line the spring-form tin with a round of parchment paper. Brush the sides with a little sunflower oil and lightly dust them with ground almonds.

Roughly break up the gluten-free biscuits and place in the bowl of a food processor. Add the ground almonds and pour in the melted butter. Using the 'pulse' button, combine these ingredients. Remove from the bowl of the food processor and press very well into the base of the prepared tin. Refrigerate while you prepare the filling.

Wash the food processor bowl and in it combine the mascarpone, ricotta, crème fraîche, eggs, caster sugar, cornflour, lemon rind and lemon juice. Mix or process the filling for a few seconds until smooth.

Remove the pulp from the passion-fruit and stir through the cheesecake mixture with half the raspberries. Pour the mixture into the spring-form tin and scatter the remaining raspberries on top.

Bake in the oven for about 45–50 minutes. The cheesecake should be set around the sides but still slightly wobbly in the centre.

Allow the cheesecake to cool in the tin and then refrigerate until it is completely cold and set overnight, if possible, for the flavours to develop. Carefully remove from the tin and serve with softly whipped cream.

Per serving: 695 kcals, 54g fat, 28g saturated fat, 43g carbohydrate, 0.26g sodium, 189mg calcium

Baked blueberry cheesecake

This variation is also utterly yummy. Omit the passion-fruit and raspberries and follow the method using 225–275g (8–10oz) blueberries.

Per serving: 695 kcals, 54g fat, 28g saturated fat, 43g carbohydrate, 0.26g sodium, 184mg calcium

Tiramisu

Having had to listen to my friends oohh and ahhh while eating tiramisu, I decided it was time to try a coeliac-friendly version. Individual tiramisus also look great and keep really well. I usually make it the day before I serve it. **Serves 8**

250ml (9fl oz) strong espresso (if not strong enough, add 1 teaspoon instant coffee)

2 tablespoons brandy

2 tablespoons Jamaica rum

75g (3oz) gluten-free dark chocolate

3 eggs, preferably free range, separated

4 tablespoons caster sugar

250g (9oz) mascarpone

1 quantity Almond Fingers (see page 129)

Unsweetened gluten-free cocoa powder, for dusting

Low-sided serving dish, 20 x 25cm (8 x 10in)

Mix the coffee with the brandy and rum. Roughly grate the chocolate (or put in a food processor and use the pulse button). Whisk the egg yolks with the sugar until the mixture reaches the 'ribbon' stage and is light and fluffy, then fold in the mascarpone, a tablespoon at a time.

Whisk the egg whites until stiff peaks form and fold gently into the egg-yolk mixture.

Line the base of the dish with a single layer of plain almond fingers. Dip each side of the next set of almond fingers very quickly into the coffee mixture and arrange side by side on top of the plain almond fingers. (The almond fingers absorb the coffee mixture very quickly and excess liquid will drain through onto the plain almond fingers below.)

Spread half the mascarpone mixture gently over the almond fingers, sprinkle half the grated chocolate on top, then another layer of plain almond fingers. Repeat with a layer of soaked almond fingers (as before) and finally the rest of the mascarpone mixture. Cover the dish with clingfilm or, better still, slide it into a plastic bag and twist the end. Refrigerate for at least 6 hours. (It will keep for several days in the fridge, but ensure it is covered so that it doesn't pick up odours.)

To serve, scatter the remaining chocolate over the top and dust with unsweetened cocoa powder.

Per serving: 587 kcals, 40g fat, 17g saturated fat, 42g carbohydrate, 0.18g sodium, 118mg calcium

Chocolate fudge pudding

Your friends will be queuing up for invitations to dinner when you serve this delectable pud. Add some freshly roasted hazelnuts and a dash of Fra Angelica to the whipped cream for extra pizazz. **Serves 6–8**

150g (5oz) best-quality gluten-free dark chocolate (70% cocoa solids)
150g (5oz) butter
1 teaspoon pure vanilla extract
150ml (¼ pint) warm water
110g (4oz) caster sugar
4 eggs, preferably free range, separated

25g (1oz) rice flour
1 teaspoon gluten-free baking powder
Gluten-free icing sugar, for dusting

1.2 litre (2 pint) pie dish or 8 individual ramekins, well greased with butter

Preheat the oven to 200°C/400°F/gas mark 6.

Cut the chocolate into small pieces and melt with the butter in a heatproof bowl over a pan of simmering water. As soon as the chocolate has melted, remove from the heat and add the vanilla extract, then stir in the warm water and sugar. Continue to mix until smooth. Lightly beat the egg yolks and whisk them into the chocolate mixture. Fold in the sifted rice flour and gluten-free baking powder, making sure there are no lumps.

Whisk the egg whites in a large, scrupulously clean bowl until stiff peaks form. Fold gently into the chocolate mixture and pour into the greased pie dish or ramekins.

Put the pie dish into a bain-marie of hot water and bake for 10 minutes (for the single dish), then reduce the temperature to 160°C/325°F/gas mark 3 for a further 20–30 minutes. If you are making individual dishes, they will be cooked in about 15 minutes at 200°C/400°F/gas mark 6. The pudding should be firm on the top but still soft and fudgy underneath. Dust with gluten-free icing sugar and serve hot, warm or cold with softly whipped cream.

Per serving: 483 kcals, 35g fat, 19g saturated fat, 37g carbohydrate, 0.34g sodium, 49mg calcium

Bread and butter pudding

This is a great way of using up leftover gluten free white bread: feel-good comfort food at its very best. Don't reduce the recipe quantities here. Just enjoy. **Serves 6–8**

12 slices of gluten-free white bread (see page 120)
50g (2oz) butter, preferably unsalted
½ teaspoon freshly grated nutmeg
200g (7oz) plump raisins or sultanas
4 large eggs, preferably free range, lightly beaten
225ml (8fl oz) milk

450 ml (16fl oz) single cream
1 teaspoon pure vanilla extract
175g (6oz) caster sugar
Pinch of salt
1 tablespoon granulated sugar, for sprinkling
Softly whipped cream, to serve

20cm (8in) square pottery or china dish

Butter the gluten-free bread and arrange 4 slices, buttered side down, in a single layer in the dish. Sprinkle the bread with half the nutmeg and half the raisins, arrange another layer of gluten-free bread, buttered side down, over the raisins and sprinkle the remaining nutmeg and raisins on top. Cover with the remaining gluten-free bread, buttered side down.

In a bowl whisk the eggs and add the milk, cream, vanilla extract, caster sugar and a pinch of salt. Pour the mixture through a fine sieve over the gluten-free bread. Sprinkle the granulated sugar over the top and let the mixture stand, covered loosely, at room temperature for at least 1 hour or chill overnight.

Preheat the oven to 180°C/350°F/gas mark 4.

Place in a bain-marie of hot water to come half way up the sides of the baking dish. Bake in the centre of the oven for about 1 hour until the top is crisp and golden. Serve warm with softly whipped cream.

Tip: You could use leftover gluten-free scones or gluten-free fruit bread instead of or as well as leftover gluten-free bread.

Per serving: 628 kcals, 29g fat, 16g saturated fat, 83g carbohydrate, 0.54g sodium, 208mg calcium

Sticky toffee pudding with hot toffee sauce

Another treat that many coeliacs feel they might have to forgo forever. The sauce keeps for months and is delicious with ice cream, or even sliced bananas. **Serves 8**

225g (8oz) dates, chopped
300ml (½ pint) hot tea
Sunflower oil
110g (4oz) rice flour
110g (4oz) tapioca flour
1½ teaspoons gluten-free
   baking powder
1 teaspoon xanthan gum
110g (4oz) unsalted butter
175g (6oz) caster sugar
3 eggs, preferably free range
1 teaspoon bicarbonate of
   soda

1 teaspoon pure vanilla extract
1 teaspoon espresso coffee
For the hot toffee sauce
110g (4oz) butter
175g (6oz) dark soft brown
   Barbados sugar
110g (4oz) granulated sugar
300g (10½oz) golden syrup
250ml (8fl oz) single cream
½ teaspoon pure vanilla extract

20cm (8in) spring-form tin
   with removable base

Preheat the oven to 180°C/350°F/gas mark 4.

Soak the dates in the tea for 15 minutes.

Brush the cake tin with sunflower oil and place a circle of oiled greaseproof paper on the base.

Sift together the flours, baking powder and xanthan gum. Cream the butter and sugar until light and soft. Beat in the eggs, one at a time, and fold in the flour mixture. Add the bicarbonate of soda, vanilla extract and espresso coffee to the dates and tea and stir this into the mixture. Turn into the prepared tin and cook for 1–1½ hours or until a skewer inserted into the centre comes out clean.

To make the sauce, put the butter, sugars and golden syrup into a heavy-based saucepan and melt gently on a low heat. Simmer for about 5 minutes, remove from the heat and gradually stir in the cream and the vanilla extract. Return to the heat and stir for 2–3 minutes until the sauce is smooth.

Pour a little sauce onto a serving plate. Put the sticky toffee pudding on top and pour over more sauce. Put the remaining sauce in a bowl to serve, along with softly whipped cream.

Per serving: 875 kcals, 35g fat, 21g saturated fat, 143g carbohydrate, 0.56g sodium, 94mg calcium

Ballymaloe mince pies with irish whiskey cream

Few of us can resist mince pies, especially when they are made with homemade mincemeat and served with whiskey-flavoured cream. **Makes 20–24**

1 quantity Rosemary's sweet pastry (see page 136)
450g (1lb) Ballymaloe mincemeat (see page 155)
Egg wash
Gluten-free icing sugar, for dusting

For the Irish whiskey cream
1 teaspoon gluten-free icing sugar
1–3 tablespoons Irish whiskey
225ml (8fl oz) softly whipped cream

Make the gluten-free sweet shortcrust pastry following the recipe and chill for 1 hour in the fridge.

Preheat the oven to 180°C/350°F/gas mark 4.

Roll out the pastry until quite thin, stamp into rounds using a 7cm (3in) cutter and line shallow bun tins. Place a good teaspoon of the mincemeat into each pastry case, dampen the edges with water and place another round of pastry on top. Use any scraps of the pastry to make leaves and holly berries for the top of the pies, then brush with egg wash.

Bake the mince pies in the oven for about 20–25 minutes. Allow them to cool slightly, and then dust with gluten-free icing sugar or caster sugar.

To make the cream, fold the sugar and whiskey into the whipped cream and serve with the warm gluten-free mince pies.

Per serving: 710 kcals, 32g fat, 16g saturated fat, 108g carbohydrate, 0.15g sodium, 66mg calcium

Christmas cake with toasted almond paste

A moist, succulent cake, which Rosemary adapted from Darina's recipe. The almond paste keeps the cake for months, but for marzipan lovers it's more delicious than fondant icing. **Serves 20**

110g (4oz) glace cherries
50g (2oz) whole almonds
350g (12oz) best-quality sultanas
350g (12oz) best-quality raisins
350g (12oz) best-quality currants
275g (10oz) ground almonds
110g (4oz) candied peel
Grated rind of 1 lemon
Grated rind of 1 orange
60ml (2½fl oz) Irish whiskey
225g (8oz) butter
225g (8oz) soft brown sugar

6 eggs, preferably free range
1 teaspoon gluten-free ground mixed spice
110g (4oz) rice flour
2 teaspoons xanthan gum
1 large Bramley's Seedling apple
Almond paste (see recipe)
1 egg white, preferably free range, lightly beaten, to brush on the cake
2 egg yolks, preferably free range, to glaze
23cm (9in) round tin or 20cm (8in) square tin

Line the base and sides of the tin with brown paper and greaseproof paper, with an outer collar of brown paper to come half as high again as the height of the tin.

Wash and dry the cherries. Cut in half or quarters as desired. Blanch the whole almonds in boiling water for 1–2 minutes, rub off the skins and chop the nuts finely. Mix the dried fruit, the chopped almonds, 50g (2oz) of the ground almonds and the grated orange and lemon rind. Add about half of the whiskey and leave for 1 hour to macerate.

Preheat the oven to 180°C/350°F/gas mark 4.

Cream the butter until very soft, add the sugar and beat until pale and light. Whisk the eggs and add bit by bit, beating well between each addition.

Mix the spice with the remaining ground almonds, the rice flour and xanthan gum and stir in gently. Grate the apple, add to the fruit and mix in gently but thoroughly (don't beat the mixture again or you will toughen the cake).

Put the mixture into the prepared cake tin. Make a slight hollow in the centre, dip your hand in water and pat it over the surface of the cake: this ensures that the top is smooth when cooked. Lay a sheet of brown paper over the top of the tin. Put into the oven and cook for 1 hour, then reduce the heat to 160°C/325°F/gas mark 3 for a further 3–3½ hours. Test by inserting a skewer into the centre: the cake is cooked if it comes out completely clean.

Pour the rest of the whiskey over the cake and leave to cool in the tin.

The following day, remove the cake from the tin but do not remove the lining paper. Wrap in extra greaseproof paper and aluminium foil until required. The cake keeps for weeks or even months at this stage.

When you are ready to cover the cake with almond paste, remove the paper from the cake. Put a sheet of greaseproof paper on the work surface and dust with some gluten-free icing sugar. Roll out about half the almond paste on the paper: it should be a little less than 1cm (½in) thick. Brush the top of the cake with the lightly beaten egg white and put the cake, sticky side down, on top of the rolled-out the almond paste.

Give the cake a 'thump' to make sure it sticks and then cut around the edge. If the cake is a little 'round shouldered', cut the almond paste a little larger; pull away the extra bits and keep for later to make hearts or holly leaves. With a palette knife press the extra almond paste in against the top of the cake to fill any gaps. Then slide a knife underneath the paper and turn the cake right way up. Peel off the paper.

Preheat the oven to 220°C/425°F/gas mark 7.

Measure the circumference of the cake with a piece of string. Roll out 2 long strips of almond paste to half that length: trim both edges to the height of the cake with a palette knife. Brush both the cake and the almond paste lightly with egg white. Press the strip against the sides of the cake: do not overlap or there will be a bulge. Use a straight-sided glass to even the edges and smooth the join. Rub the cake well with your hand to ensure a nice flat surface. Roll out the remainder of the almond paste to about 5mm (¼in) thick. Cut out decorative shapes, brush the whole surface of the cake with beaten egg yolk, and stick the shapes at intervals around the sides and top of the cake. Brush these with egg yolk too.

Carefully lift the cake onto a baking sheet and bake for 15–20 minutes or until just slightly toasted. Remove from the oven, allow to cool and then transfer to a cake board.

Per serving: 491 kcals, 23g fat, 8g saturated fat, 67g carbohydrate, 0.17g sodium, 116mg calcium

Almond paste

450g (1lb) ground almonds
450g (1lb) caster sugar, sifted
2 small eggs, preferably free
  range

Drop of pure almond essence
2 tablespoons Irish whiskey
Gluten-free icing sugar

Mix the ground almonds with the sifted sugar. Beat the eggs, add in the whiskey and 1 drop of the almond essence, then add to the other ingredients and mix to a stiff paste. (You may not need all of the egg). Sprinkle the work surface with gluten-free icing sugar, turn out the almond paste and work lightly until smooth.

Per serving: 541 kcals, 30g fat, 3g saturated fat, 56g carbohydrate, 0.03g sodium, 137mg calcium

Basic Recipes

8

Pesto
This takes minutes to make and tastes a million times better than most pesto you buy. If you can't get hold of enough basil, you can use parsley, a mixture of parsley and mint, or parsley and coriander. **Makes 2 jars**

110g (4oz) fresh basil leaves
150–225ml (5–8fl oz) extra
   virgin olive oil
25g (1oz) fresh pine kernels
   (if possible, taste before you
   buy to be sure they are not
   rancid)

2 large garlic cloves, crushed
50g (2oz) finely grated
   Parmesan cheese
Salt, to taste

Whiz the basil with the olive oil, pine kernels and garlic in a food processor or pound using a pestle and mortar. Transfer to a bowl and fold in the finely grated Parmesan cheese. Taste and season.

Serve with pasta, goat's cheese, tomato and mozzarella. Pesto is great in salads or sprinkled over omelettes or frittata. It keeps for weeks, covered with a layer of olive oil in a jar in the fridge, and also freezes well, but for best results don't add the grated Parmesan until it has defrosted. Freeze in small batches for convenience. Basil leaves also freeze very well; they won't be great for pesto but can be used in soups and vegetable stews to add a summer zing.

Per recipe: 1687 kcals, 171g fat, 31g saturated fat, 9g carbohydrate, 1.34g sodium, 918mg calcium

Mint and parsley pesto
Substitute 50g (2oz) fresh mint and 50g (2oz) fresh parsley for the basil in the above recipe.

Yorkshire pudding
You now no longer need to forgo those delicious Yorkshire puds – here Rosemary uses rice and tapioca flour with great success. For a twist, add a few thyme leaves, a blob of Dijon mustard or a few olives. **Serves 8–10**

50g (2oz) rice flour
50g (2oz) tapioca flour
Pinch of salt
2 eggs, preferably free range
300ml (½ pint) milk

10g (½oz) butter, melted
Olive oil or pure beef dripping
   (unless for vegetarians), for
   greasing tins
Deep bun tin

Preheat the oven to 230°C/450°F/gas mark 8.
Sift the rice flour and tapioca flour into a large bowl. Add the salt. Make a well in the centre and drop in the eggs. Using a small whisk or wooden spoon, stir continuously, gradually drawing in flour from the sides, adding half the milk in a steady stream at the same time. When all the flour has been mixed in, whisk in the remainder of the milk and the cool melted butter. Allow to stand for 1 hour.
Grease a hot deep bun tin with olive oil or beef dripping and fill up to half to two thirds with the batter. Bake in the oven for about 20 minutes. Remove from the tins and serve warm.

Per serving: 132 kcals, 8g fat, 2g saturated fat, 13g carbohydrate, 0.15g sodium, 56mg calcium

American popovers
You can convert the individual Yorkshire puddings into American popovers and serve as a sweet treat. Simply put a blob of softly whipped cream and a spoonful of homemade raspberry or blackcurrant jam into the centre of each popover. Sprinkle with gluten-free icing sugar and serve.

Pizza base

There'll be no stopping you once you've made your first gluten-free pizza dough. Pizza is universally appealing, a quick and easy lunch or supper dish, for which you can endlessly vary the toppings. **Makes 4 pizzas**

1 teaspoon sugar
225ml (8fl oz) lukewarm water
15g (½oz) dried active yeast
175g (6oz) rice flour, plus extra for dusting
75g (3oz) potato flour
50g (2oz) tapioca flour

25g (1oz) dried milk
1½ teaspoons gluten-free baking powder
1 teaspoon xanthan gum
1 teaspoon salt
1 tablespoon sunflower oil
1 egg, preferably free range

Dissolve the sugar in 150ml (¼ pint) of the lukewarm water in a small bowl and stir in the dried yeast. Sit the bowl for a few minutes in a warm place to allow the yeast to start to work. After about 4–5 minutes it will have a creamy, slightly frothy appearance.

Place the rice flour, potato flour, tapioca flour, dried milk, gluten-free baking powder, xanthan gum and salt into the bowl of a food mixer. Using the paddle attachment, thoroughly mix the dry ingredients together. In a small bowl, whisk together the sunflower oil and egg and stir into the dry ingredients on a low speed.

When the yeast mixture is ready, stir and pour with the remaining lukewarm water into the mixer bowl. Using the K-blade attachment on a low speed, mix the liquid through the contents of the bowl. Continue to mix for 3–4 minutes, until a smooth dough is produced.

Transfer the dough to a rice-floured work surface. The dough will be slightly sticky, so it helps if you put a little rice flour on your hands too. Divide the dough into 4 equal pieces, each weighing about 150g (5oz). Place a sheet of parchment paper on a baking tray. Transfer 1 piece of the dough to the baking tray and, using the 'heel' of your hand, flatten it to form a circle measuring 20cm (8in) in diameter. Repeat with the remaining 3 pieces of dough.

Cover the dough circles with a clean tea-towel and allow them to rise in a warm place for about 15 minutes.

Preheat the oven to 200°C/400°F/gas mark 6.

Transfer the baking sheets to the oven and bake for 8–10 minutes before removing and adding the toppings of your choice. Return the pizzas, with the toppings to the oven and bake for a further 10–15 minutes until the bases are crisp and the toppings are bubbly and golden.

Serve immediately.

Per pizza: 348 kcals, 7g fat, 2g saturated fat, 67g carbohydrate, 0.78g sodium, 123mg calcium

Gluten-free roux
Gluten-free roux works just as effectively to thicken flour-based sauces, and occasionally gravies, as regular flour-based roux. Have some in the fridge: it will keep for up to a fortnight. Make it in small or large quantities for future use.

110g (4oz) butter
50g (2oz) cornflour
50g (2oz) rice flour

Melt the butter in a saucepan and add the cornflour and rice flour. Combine the mixture with a wooden spoon and cook for 2 minutes on a low heat, stirring occasionally.

Per recipe: 1265 kcals, 103g fat, 65g saturated fat, 86g carbohydrate, 0.97g sodium, 38mg calcium

Gluten-free béchamel sauce
Classic béchamel sauce starts by making a roux and gradually adding milk, whisking all the time to avoid lumps. However, if you have some gluten-free roux prepared, simply whisk into the boiling milk.

600ml (1 pint) milk
Few slices of carrot and onion
3 black peppercorns
Sprig of thyme
4 parsley stalks
50g (2oz) butter
25g (1oz) cornflour
25g (1oz) rice flour
Salt and freshly ground black pepper

Put the milk into a saucepan with the carrot, onion, peppercorns, thyme and parsley. Bring to the boil, simmer for 4–5 minutes, remove from the heat and cool. Strain the vegetables.
Melt the butter in a saucepan and stir in the cornflour and rice flour. Combine the mixture with a wooden spoon and cook for 2 minutes over a low heat. Pour in the milk, whisking continuously, and allow to thicken. Taste for seasoning and adjust if necessary.
For a thinner sauce, add a little extra milk until you achieve the required consistency.

Per recipe: 823 kcals, 51g fat, 32g saturated fat, 74g carbohydrate, 1.51g sodium, 746mg calcium

Rosemary's savoury pastry
Gluten-free flours are a little harder to work with, but worth mastering. Keep the dough dry; although slightly more difficult to handle, it gives a crisper, 'shorter' crust for quiches and pies. **Makes 425g (15oz)**

75g (3oz) rice flour
75g (3oz) fine cornmeal (polenta)
75g (3oz) potato flour, plus extra for dusting
1 heaped teaspoon xanthan gum
Pinch of salt
150g (5oz) butter
1 egg, preferably free range, mixed with 2 tablespoons cold water

Sift the rice flour, fine cornmeal, potato flour, xanthan gum and salt into a bowl and mix well. Cut the butter into cubes and gently rub into the flour mixture. Make a well in the centre and carefully add some of the egg and water mixture – just enough to bring the pastry together using a fork. Collect the pastry into a ball with your hands. This way you can judge more accurately whether you need a few more drops of liquid. It is tempting to add extra liquid at this stage but try not to, as it is very easy to make the pastry too wet. It is fine to have some liquid left over. Although rather damp pastry is easier to handle and roll out, the resulting crust can be tough and may well shrink out of shape in the oven.
On a very lightly rice-floured board, gently knead the dough with the heel of your hand for a few minutes to form a silky-smooth ball. Flatten slightly, wrap in clingfilm and refrigerate for about 30 minutes. This will make the pastry much less elastic and easier to roll.
When it has chilled enough, roll it out (between 2 sheets of parchment paper, if necessary, to stop it sticking) and use as required.

Per recipe: 1964 kcals, 132g fat, 80g saturated fat, 180g carbohydrate, 2.04g sodium, 116mg calcium

Savoury pancake batter
Adding melted butter to the batter makes all the difference to the flavour and texture of the pancakes and will make it possible to cook them without greasing the pan each time. **Makes 16 pancakes**

175g (6oz) tapioca flour	4 large eggs, preferably free
175g (6oz) rice flour	range, lightly beaten
½ teaspoon salt	350ml (12fl oz) milk
	4 tablespoons melted butter

Sift the tapioca flour, rice flour and salt into a large bowl. Make a well in the centre and drop in the lightly beaten eggs. Using a whisk and starting in the centre, mix the eggs gradually bringing in the flour mixture. Add the milk slowly and beat until the batter is smooth and covered in bubbles.

Refrigerate the pancake batter for at least 1 hour. Just before you cook the pancakes, whisk the batter again, as some of the flour will have settled to the bottom, and stir in the melted butter.

To cook the pancakes, heat a heavy cast-iron crêpe pan or a 20–23cm (8–9in) non-stick frying pan until very hot. Using a ladle, pour in just enough batter to cover the base of the pan thinly. Loosen the pancake around the edge, flip over with a spatula or a thin-bladed fish slice, cook for 1–2 seconds on the other side and slide off the pan onto a plate.

The pancakes may be stacked on top of each other and peeled apart later. Alternatively, they will keep in the fridge for several days or, if a disc of parchment paper is placed between each pancake, they freeze perfectly.

Per pancake: 135 kcals, 5g fat, 3g saturated fat, 20g carbohydrate, 0.12g sodium, 39mg calcium

Sweet pancakes
Add 2 tablespoons caster sugar and 1 teaspoon freshly grated lemon rind (optional) to the batter. Serve with chocolate spread and sliced bananas – or any filling of your choice.

Mushroom à la crème
This recipe is fantastically versatile. Try it as a vegetable, a filling for pancakes or omelettes, as a pasta sauce, an enrichment for stews or, by adding extra cream or stock, served as a sauce for beef, lamb, chicken or veal. **Serves 4**

15–25g (½–1oz) butter	125ml (4fl oz) single cream
75g (3oz) onions, finely	Gluten-free roux (see page
chopped	150)
225g (8oz) mushrooms, sliced	Freshly chopped parsley
Salt and freshly ground black	½ tablespoon freshly chopped
pepper	chives (optional)
Squeeze of lemon juice	

Melt the butter in a heavy sauté pan until it foams. Add the chopped onions, cover and sweat on a low heat for about 5–10 minutes or until quite soft but not coloured. Transfer the onions to a bowl.

Cook the mushrooms in a hot frying pan, in batches if necessary. Season each batch with salt, freshly ground pepper and a tiny squeeze of lemon juice. Add the onions to the mushrooms in the pan, then add the cream and allow to bubble for a few minutes. Crumble in a little roux and boil to thicken slightly. Taste and adjust the seasoning if necessary, and add parsley and chives, if using. Mushroom à la crème keeps well in the fridge for 4–5 days.

Per serving: 422 kcals, 35g fat, 22g saturated fat, 25g carbohydrate, 0.39g sodium, 51mg calcium

Mushroom à la crème with ginger and toasted almonds
Add 1 teaspoon freshly grated ginger and 20g (¾oz) lightly toasted nibbed almonds with the cream.

Mushroom and rosemary sauce
Add 1–2 tablespoons freshly chopped rosemary to the sautéed mushrooms in the master recipe. Add the cream, taste and adjust the seasoning if necessary.

Homemade vegetable stock
This is only a guide: you can make stock from whatever veg you have available, but don't let the flavour of any one vegetable predominate, unless you want it to. **Makes about 1.8 litres (3 pints)**

1 small white turnip
2 onions, roughly sliced
Green parts of 2–3 leeks
3 celery sticks (use the outside ones), washed and roughly chopped
3 large carrots, scrubbed and roughly chopped

½ fennel bulb, roughly chopped
75g (3oz) mushrooms or mushroom stalks
4–6 parsley stalks
Bouquet garni
Few black peppercorns
2.4 litres (4 pints) cold water

Put all the ingredients into a large pan, bring to the boil, then reduce the heat, cover and simmer for 1–1½ hours. Strain the stock before use, or keep for a week in the fridge or freeze it.

Per recipe: 4 kcals, 0g fat, 0g saturated fat, 0g carbohydrate, 0.18g sodium, 19mg calcium

Homemade beef stock
Planning ahead is the key to making stock. Keep your bones for the stock pot – or ask your butcher or supermarket for some. Homemade stock is both tastier and healthier as it contains less salt. **Makes about 4 litres (7 pints)**

2.2–2.6kg (5–6lb) beef bones, preferably with meat on, cut into small pieces
2 large onions, quartered
2 large carrots, quartered
2 celery sticks, chopped

Large bouquet garni
10 peppercorns
2 cloves
4 garlic cloves, unpeeled
1 teaspoon tomato purée
5 litres (8¾ pints) water

Preheat the oven to 230°C/450°F/gas mark 8. Put the bones into a roasting tin and roast for 30 minutes until well browned.

Add the vegetables and return to the oven until they are also browned. Transfer everything to a stock pot. Add the bouquet garni, spices, garlic and tomato purée. Degrease the tin and deglaze with some of the water, bring to the boil and pour into the stock pot. Add the rest of the water and bring slowly to the boil. Skim off the fat and simmer gently for 5–6 hours. Strain, cool, and skim off any remaining fat off before use.

Per recipe: 4 kcals, 0g fat, 0g saturated fat, 0g carbohydrate, 0.18g sodium, 19mg calcium

Homemade chicken stock

The French word for stock means foundation and indeed it is the foundation of many recipes, essential in soups, stews and many sauces. Never discard a carcass without making stock! **Makes 3 litres (5 pints)**

2–3 raw or cooked chicken carcasses or a mixture of both

Giblets from the chicken (neck, heart, gizzard, but save the liver for another dish)

About 3.6 litres (6 pints) cold water

1 large onion, sliced

1 leek (optional) – use the green parts; keep the white as a vegetable

1 outside celery stick or 1 lovage leaf

1 large carrot, sliced

Few parsley stalks

Sprig of thyme

6 black peppercorns

Chop up the carcasses as much as possible. Put all the ingredients into a large saucepan or stock pot and cover with the water. Bring to the boil and skim the fat off the top with a tablespoon. Simmer for 2–3 hours. Strain, cool and remove any remaining fat. If you need a stronger flavour, boil down the liquid in an open pan to reduce the volume by one-third or one-half. Do not add salt.

The above recipe is just a guideline. If you have only one carcass and can't be bothered to make a small quantity of stock, why not freeze it and save up until you have 6 or 7 carcasses plus giblets? Then you can celebrate and make a really decent-sized pot of stock and get best value for your time and energy!

Per recipe: 4 kcals, 0g fat, 0g saturated fat, 0g carbohydrate, 0.18g sodium, 19mg calcium

Notes

Stock keeps for several days in the fridge. If you need to keep it longer, boil it up again for 5–6 minutes every couple of days; allow it to cool and refrigerate again. Stock also freezes well. Large yogurt cartons or plastic milk bottles make inexpensive containers; you can then cut them off the frozen stock if you need to defrost it in a hurry!

In restaurants the stock is usually allowed to simmer uncovered to make it as clear as possible, but you may prefer to keep the pot covered, otherwise the entire house will smell of stock.

Chicken liver should not go into the pot because it makes the stock bitter. Save the livers to make a delicious smooth pâté.

Some vegetables which should not be used for stock:
Potatoes soak up flavour and make the stock cloudy.
Parsnips are too strong.
Beetroot are also too strong and the dye would produce a red stock – but make beetroot soup instead!
Cabbage or other brassicas give an off-taste on long cooking.
White turnip – a little is sometimes an asset, but it is very easy to overdo.
Bay leaf has a flavour that can easily predominate in chicken stock and add a sameness to soups made from the stock.

Salt is another ingredient that you will find in most stock recipes, but not here. The reason is that if you want to reduce the stock to make a sauce, it very soon becomes over-salted.

Fresh mint chutney

This fresh chutney is often served with curries. It makes a really yummy dip with poppadoms before dinner as a simple starter. It is also good with grilled fish or roast lamb instead of mint sauce. **Serves 6**

1 large cooking apple (we use Grenadier or Bramley's Seedling), peeled and cored
Large handful of fresh mint leaves (Spearmint or Bowles)
50g (2oz) onions
25–50g (1–2oz) caster sugar (depending on the tartness of the apple)
Salt and cayenne pepper

Whiz all the ingredients in a food processor, then season with the salt and a little cayenne.

Per serving: 36 kcals, 0g fat, 0g saturated fat, 9g carbohydrate, 0.1g sodium, 13mg calcium

Tsatsiki

This is a popular Greek dip that can be served as part of a mezze, as an accompanying salad or as a sauce with grilled fish or meat. Greek yogurt is usually made with sheep's milk and is wonderfully thick and creamy.

1 crisp cucumber, peeled and cut into 3–5mm (⅛–¼in) dice
Salt and freshly ground black pepper
1–2 garlic cloves, crushed
Dash of white wine vinegar or lemon juice
425ml (¾ pint) Greek yogurt or best-quality natural yogurt
4 tablespoons whipping cream (optional)
1 heaped tablespoon freshly chopped mint
Sugar

Put the cucumber dice in a sieve, sprinkle with salt and allow to drain for about 30 minutes. Dry the cucumber on kitchen paper, put into a bowl and mix with the garlic, vinegar or lemon juice, yogurt and cream, if using. Stir in the mint and taste. It may need seasoning with salt, pepper and a little sugar.

Per recipe (without cream): 577 kcals, 41g fat, 26g saturated fat, 20g carbohydrate, 0.73g sodium, 770mg calcium

Tomato fondue

Tomato fondue is one of the most important basic recipes and is infinitely versatile. Serve it as a vegetable dish, or a sauce for pasta, filling for omelettes, topping for pizza, a base for bean stews. **Serves 6**

2 tablespoons extra virgin olive oil
110g (4oz) onions, sliced
1 garlic clove, crushed
900g (2lb) very ripe tomatoes, peeled, in summer, or 2½ x 400g (14oz) tins tomatoes in winter
Salt, freshly ground black pepper and sugar to taste
1 tablespoon any of the following: freshly chopped mint or torn basil or a mixture of thyme, parsley, lemon balm and marjoram
Balsamic vinegar

Heat the oil in a heavy-based cast-iron or stainless-steel saucepan. Add the onions and garlic, toss until coated, cover and sweat on a gentle heat until soft but not coloured. It is vital for the success of this dish that the onions are completely soft before the tomatoes are added. Slice the peeled fresh or tinned tomatoes and add with all the juice to the onions.
Season with salt, freshly ground pepper and sugar (tinned tomatoes need lots of sugar because of their high acidity). Add the herbs. Cook, covered, for 10 minutes. Remove the lid and continue to cook for about 10 minutes more, or until the tomato softens. Cook fresh tomatoes for a shorter time to preserve the lively fresh flavour. Tinned tomatoes need to be cooked for longer depending on whether you want to use the fondue as a vegetable, sauce or filling.
Add a few drops of balsamic vinegar at the end of cooking to greatly enhance the flavour.

Per serving: 74 kcals, 4g fat, 1g saturated fat, 8g carbohydrate, 0.11g sodium, 21mg calcium

Variations
Add 1–2 chopped fresh chillies to the sweating onions.
Substitute 2–3 tablespoons of freshly chopped coriander for the other herbs in the recipe. Good with or without chilli.

Sun-dried tomatoes
Sun-dried tomatoes preserved in olive oil are now common in shops and delis, but you can make your own if you have a 4-door Aga – and a fan oven also works well. Use on salads, with gluten-free pasta, or as a snack.

Very ripe tomatoes	Sugar
Sea salt	Olive oil

Cut the tomatoes in half across the equator, put them on a wire rack, season with sea salt and sugar and drizzle with olive oil. Leave in the coolest part of a 4-door Aga, or in a fan oven set to its minimum temperature, until they are totally dried out and wizened. Leave them in for 24 hours, depending on size (after about 1 hour turn them upside down).

Store in sterilised jars covered with olive oil. A few basil leaves or a couple of sprigs of rosemary, thyme or annual marjoram added to the oil make them especially delicious. Cover and keep in a cool, dry, preferably dark place.

Alternatively, for oven-roasted tomatoes, proceed as above but remove and the use tomatoes while they are still plump but have reduced in size by half.

Per tomato: 24 kcals, 1g fat, 0g saturated fat, 3g carbohydrate, 0.11g sodium, 6mg calcium

Garlic butter
Flavoured butters can be rolled into butter pats or formed into a log and wrapped in greaseproof paper or aluminium foil, with each end screwed so that it looks like a cracker. Refrigerate to harden. It will keep for 2–3 weeks.

110g (4oz) butter, softened	3–5 garlic cloves, crushed
2 tablespoons finely chopped parsley	Few drops freshly squeezed lemon juice

Cream the butter and add the parsley, crushed garlic and a few drops of lemon juice. Roll into a log and use as required.

Per recipe: 940 kcals, 102g fat, 65g saturated fat, 3g carbohydrate, 0.94g sodium, 42mg calcium

Ballymaloe mincemeat
Homemade mincemeat is extremely easy to prepare and can be made well in advance of Christmas. This recipe will keep for up to a year in a cool, airy place. **Makes 3.5kg (7¾lb)**

2 cooking apples (we use Bramley's Seedling)	2 tablespoons orange marmalade
2 lemons	225g (8oz) currants
450g (1lb) gluten-free minced beef suet or butter, chilled and grated	450g (1lb) raisins
	225g (8oz) sultanas
110g (4oz) mixed peel, preferably homemade	900g (2lb) dark, soft, brown Barbados sugar
	60ml (2½fl oz) Irish whiskey

Preheat the oven to. 180°C/350°F/gas mark 4.

Core the apples and bake whole for about 45 minutes. Allow to cool, then remove the skin and mash the flesh into pulp.

Finely grate the rind from the lemons and squeeze out the juice. Add apple pulp and the remaining ingredients, mixing thoroughly between each addition. Put into clean, sterilised jars, cover with jam covers and leave to mature for 2 weeks before using.

Per rounded tablespoon: 82 kcals, 3g fat, 1g saturated fat, 14g carbohydrate, 0.01g sodium, 8mg calcium

Watercress butter

110 g (4oz) butter	Few drops of freshly squeezed lemon juice
2–4 tablespoons finely chopped watercress leaves	

Cream the butter and add in the watercress and a few drops of lemon juice. Roll into butter pats or form into a log (see garlic butter, left) and refrigerate to harden.

Per recipe: 814 kcals, 90g fat, 57g saturated fat, 0g carbohydrate, 0.83g sodium, 42mg calcium

Resources

The various coeliac societies, depending upon where you live in the country, are probably your best bet for getting information about coeliacs. They will be able to put you in touch with local groups, and inform you about up and coming events that would be of interest to coeliacs whether you are newly diagnosed or an existing member. They also increase awareness within the food industry and fund research into the coeliac condition.

AUSTRALIA

The Coeliac Society of NSW
PO Box 703, Chatswood NSW 2057
Tel: +61 2 9411 4100
info@nsw.coeliac.org.au
www.nsw.coeliac.org.au
The Coeliac Society of Tasmania Inc
PO Box 159, Launceston 7250, Tasmania
Tel: +61 3 6344 4279
qpetas@bigpond.net.au www.coeliac.org.au
Northern Territory, c/o C.S. of South Australia
Unit 5, 88 Glynburn Road, Hectorville 5073, South Australia
Tel: +61 8 8365 1488
verus@topend.com.au
Coeliac Society of Western Australia
PO Box 1344, East Victoria Park WA 6981, Western Australia
Tel: +61 8 9470 4122
coeliacwa@bigpond.com
www.wa.coeliac.org.au
Coeliac Society of Victoria Inc
PO Box 89, Holmesglen 3148, Victoria
Tel: +61 3 9808 5566
dbaker_csv@hotkey.net.au
www.coeliac.org.au
Coeliac Society of South Australia Inc
5/88 Glynburn Road, Hectorville 5073, South Australia
Tel: +61 8 8365 1488
coeliac_society_sa@bigpond.com
www.coeliac.org.au
The Queensland Coeliac Society Inc
PO Box 2110, Fortitude Valley BC 4006, Queensland
Tel: +61 7 3854 0123
coelqld@webexpress.net.au
www.qld.coeliac.org.au

CANADA

Canadian Celiac Association
5170 Dixie Road, Suite 204,
Mississauga L4W 1E3, Ontario
Tel: +1 905 507 6208
celiac@look.ca
www.celiac.ca
Fondation Quebecoise de la Maladie Coeliaque
4837 rue Boyer, Bureau 230,
Montreal H2J 3E6, Quebec
Tel: +1 514 529 8806
info@fqmc.org
www.fqmc.org

IRELAND

The Coeliac Society of Ireland
Carmichael Centre, 4 North Brunswick Street, Dublin 7
Tel: +353 1872 1471
coeliac@iol.ie
www.coeliac.ie

NEW ZEALAND

Coeliac Society of New Zealand (Inc)
PO Box 35724, Browns Bay,
AUCKLAND 1330
Tel: +64 9 820 5157
coeliac@xtra.co.nz

SOUTH AFRICA

Coeliac Society of South Africa
PO Box 64203, Highlands North,
2037 Johannesburg
Tel: +27 11 440 3431
coeliac@netactive.co.za

SPAIN

F.A.C.E.
C/Lanuza, 19 Local Izquierdo, 28028 Madrid
Tel: +34 91 713 01 47
celiacos@teleline.es
www.celiacos.org
S.M.A.P.
Celiacs de Catalunya

Comtal 32 5e 1a, 08002 Barcelona
Tel: +34 93 412 17 89
info@celiacscatalunya.org
www.celiacscatalunya.org
F.A.C.E. - E.Z.E. Asociacion Celiaca de Euskadi
Somera 3- 3 Depto 2, Bilbao E-48005
Tel: +34 94 416 94 80
Asociacion de Padres de Celiacos de la Provincia de Las Palmas
Apartado 4237,
35080 - Las Palmas de Gran Canaria
Tel: +928 550454
asocepa@hotmail.com

UNITED KINGDOM

Coeliac UK
PO Box 220, High Wycombe,
Buckinghamshire, HP11 2HY
Tel: +44 1494 437278
admin@coeliac.co.uk
www.coeliac.co.uk

USA

Celiac Disease Foundation
13251 Ventura Boulevard, Suite 1, Studio City
91604-1838, California
Tel: +1 818 990 2354
cdf@celiac.org
http://www.celiac.org
Celiac Sprue Association/United States of America, Inc.
PO Box 31700, OMAHA 68131, Nebraska
Tel: +1 402 558 0600
celiacs@csaceliacs.org
www.csaceliacs.org
Gluten Intolerance Group
15110 10th Ave SW, Suite A,
Seattle WA 98166-1820, Washington State
Tel: +1 206 246 6652
gig@gluten.net
www.gluten.net
American Celiac Society Dietary Support Coalition
PO Box 23455, New Orleans,
LA 70183-0455
Tel: +1 504 737 3293
americanceliacsociety@yahoo.com

If you are unable to obtain gluten-free products at your local shop or health food store, contact the manufacturers directly:

AUSTRALIA
Organic Options
www.alchemix.com.au/organic.htm

SOUTH AFRICA
Diana Swales (Capetown)
dianaswales@xsinet.co.za

Healthy Life
The Pavillion, Durban

Pick and Pay Hypermarket
By-the-Sea, Durban North

Seadoone Meat Market
8a Seadoone Mall, Doonside, Amanzimtoti, Durban

The Earth Worm
63 Umhlanga Rocks Dv., Durban North

Cresta Health Shop
2 Nedbank Cresta Centre. DF Malan Dv., Blackheath, Johannesburg

Organic World Import and Export
PO Box 2804, Honeydew, 2040, Johannesburg
www.organicworld.co.za

UNITED KINGDOM
Pleniday
Brewhurst HF Supplies Ltd,
Abbot Close, Oyster Lane, Byfleet,
Surrey KT14 7JP
Tel: 01932 354 211

Orgran
Community Foods, Micross,
Brent Terrace, London NW2 1LT
Tel: 020 8450 9411
email@community foods.co.uk
www.communityfoods.co.uk
Gluten-free pasta

Ener-G
General Dietary Ltd, PO Box 38,
Kingston-upon-Thames, Surrey KT2 7YP
Tel: 020 8336 2323
Pure rice bran

Barkat, Glutano, Tritamyl, Valpiform
Gluten Free Foods Ltd, Unit 270,
Centennial Park, Centennial Avenue,
Elstree, Borehamwood, Herts. WD6 3SS
Tel: 020 8953 4444
info@glutenfree-foods.co.uk
www.glutenfree-foods.co.uk

Pure
Innovative Solutions UK Ltd,
Tunstall Road, Bosley, Nr Macclesfield,
Cheshire SK11 0PE
Tel: 0845 601 3151

Bi-Aglut
Novartis Consumer Health,
Wimblehurst Road, Horsham,
West Sussex RH12 5AB
Tel: 0845 601 2665

Glutafin, Rite-Diet, Trufree
Nutricia Dietary Care, Newmarket Avenue,
White Horse Business Park, Trowbridge,
Wiltshire BA14 0XQ
Tel: 01225 711801
glutenfree@nutricia.co.uk
www.glutafin.co.uk

Dietary Specialties, Schar
Nutrition Point Ltd, 13 Taurus Park,
Westbrook, Warrington WA5 5ZT
Tel: 07041 544044
info@nutritionpoint.ltd.uk
www.glutenfree-dsdirect.co.uk

Juvela
SHS International, 100 Wavertree Boulevard,
Wavertree Technology Park, Liverpool L7 9PT
Tel: 0151 228 1992
info@shsint.co.uk
www.shsweb.co.uk

Aproten, Arnotts, Lifestyle Healthcare, Ultra
Ultrapharm Ltd, Centenary Business Park,
Henley-on-Thames, Oxon RG9 1DS
Tel: 01491 570 000

Lifestyle Health Care Ltd
Centenary Business Park,
Henley-on-Thames, Oxon RG9 1DS
Tel: 01491 570000
www.gfdiet.com
Naturally occurring gluten-free flours and xanthan gum including the Allergycare range

Doves Farm Foods
Hungerford, Berkshire RG17 0RF
Tel: 01488 684880
www.dovesfarm.co.uk
Naturally occurring gluten-free flours

Goodness Direct
South March, Daventry,
Northants NN11 4PH
Tel: 0871 871 6611
www.GoodnessDirect.co.uk
Xanthan gum and naturally occurring gluten-free flours

USA
Ener-G
www.ener-g.com

The Gluten-Free Mall
www.GlutenFreeMall.com

Gluten Solutions
www.glutensolutions.com

Shop Natural
www.shopnatural.com

Index

First published in Great Britain 2004 by
Kyle Cathie Limited
122 Arlington Road
London NW1 7HP
general.enquiries@kyle-cathie.com
www.kylecathie.com

10 9 8 7 6 5

ISBN 1 85626 542 0

Darina Allen and Rosemary Kearney are hereby identified as the authors of this work in accordance with Section 77 of the Copyright, Designs and Patents Act 1988.

Text © 2004 Darina Allen and Rosemary Kearney
Photography © 2004 Will Heap
Book design © 2004 Kyle Cathie Limited

Senior Editor Muna Reyal
Designer Carl Hodson
Photographer Will Heap
Home economist Annie Nichols
Styling Penny Markham
Copyeditor Stephanie Horner
Editorial assistant Jennifer Wheatley
Recipe analysis Dr Wendy Doyle
Production Sha Huxtable

A Cataloguing In Publication record for this title is available from the British Library.

Colour reproduction by Sang Choy
Printed and bound in Singapore by Star Standard